The Devil is a Travelling Man

DATE DUE

The Devil is a Travelling Man

Two Plays by W.O. Mitchell

**Edited by Ormond Mitchell and
Barbara Mitchell**

Milestones in Canadian Literature

OXFORD
UNIVERSITY PRESS

OXFORD
UNIVERSITY PRESS

70 Wynford Drive, Don Mills, Ontario M3C 1J9
www.oupcanada.com

Oxford University Press is a department of the University of Oxford.
It furthers the University's objective of excellence in research, scholarship,
and education by publishing worldwide in

Oxford   New York

Auckland   Cape Town   Dar es Salaam   Hong Kong   Karachi   Kuala Lumpur   Madrid
Melbourne   Mexico City   Nairobi   New Delhi   Shanghai   Taipei   Toronto

With offices in

Argentina   Austria   Brazil   Chile   Czech Republic   France   Greece   Guatemala
Hungary   Italy   Japan   Poland   Portugal   Singapore   South Korea   Switzerland
Thailand   Turkey   Ukraine   Vietnam

Oxford is a trade mark of Oxford University Press in the UK and in certain other countries

Published in Canada by Oxford University Press

Library and Archives Canada Cataloguing in Publication

Mitchell, W. O. (William Ormond), 1914–1998
The devil is a travelling man : two plays / by W.O.
Mitchell ; Ormond Mitchell, Barbara Mitchell, editors.

(Milestones in Canadian literature)
Includes bibliographical references.
ISBN 978-0-19-543004-2

I. Mitchell, Ormond   II. Mitchell, Barbara, 1944–   III. Title.
IV. Series: Milestones in Canadian literature
PS8526.I9765D48 2009   C812'.54   C2008-908047-5

Cover image: "Autumn Carpet," Watercolour, 22x30, by Barbara Sutherland.

1 2 3 4 - 12 11 10 09

Oxford University Press is committed to our environment. This book is printed on
Forest Stewardship Council certified paper which contains 30% post-consumer waste.
Printed and bound in Canada.

W.O. Mitchell is best known for his first novel, *Who Has Seen the Wind* (1947), a Canadian classic that has sold over three-quarters of a million copies to date and is taught in schools and universities across Canada. His other novels include *The Kite* (1962), *The Vanishing Point* (1973), *How I Spent My Summer Holidays* (1981), *Since Daisy Creek* (1984), *Ladybug, Ladybug...* (1988), *Roses Are Difficult Here* (1990), *For Art's Sake* (1992), and *The Black Bonspiel of Willie MacCrimmon* (1993). *How I Spent My Summer Holidays*, hailed by some critics as his finest novel, was a best-seller, as were *The Vanishing Point, Since Daisy Creek,* and *Ladybug, Ladybug....* His "Jake and the Kid" stories first appeared in *Maclean's* in the 1940s, and in 1950 he began writing the CBC *Jake and the Kid* radio series which ran for six years and included 200 episodes. Two collections of the Jake stories were published—*Jake and the Kid* in 1961, which has sold over a quarter of a million copies, and *According to Jake and the Kid* in 1991. Both of these collections won the Stephen Leacock Award for Humour. A collection of his performance pieces, *An Evening with W.O. Mitchell*, was published in 1997. He wrote a number of stage plays, the best known of which are *Back to Beulah*, which won the Chalmers Canadian Play Award in 1976; *The Kite*; and *The Black Bonspiel of Wullie MacCrimmon*, which has had over seventy productions in Canada over the past thirty years. W.O. was appointed an Officer of the Order of Canada in 1973 and became an Honourable Member of the Privy Council in 1992.

CONTENTS

INTRODUCTION

THE BLACK BONSPIEL OF WULLIE MacCRIMMON

The precariousness of freelance writing led W.O. Mitchell to jokingly call himself the great rerun king: "The only way I've managed to stay solvent over the years was by working in several media and using the same thing over and over again...If you are confident about what you're doing and if you can remain objective about work, it's pretty good being a rerun king."[1] The story of Wullie MacCrimmon's curling duel with the Devil strikingly displays Mitchell's versatile adaptive talents. It began as a short story written around 1947, although never published as such,[2] and over the next forty-five years Mitchell adapted it into almost every other medium—radio, television, stage, and finally, in 1993, a novella.

It is as a stage play that *The Black Bonspiel of Wullie MacCrimmon* has led, and continues to lead, its most popular life. Its first production was in 1966 by the Lakefield College School. Andy Harris, a teacher at the school, adapted the television screenplay (which had just been published in Macmillan's *Three Worlds of Drama*) as the

---

[1] W.O. Mitchell, interviewed by Sid Adilman, *Toronto Star*, September 25, 1976.
[2] Only an incomplete version of this story exists in the W.O. Mitchell fonds, Msc 19. 18. 13, Special Collections, University of Calgary Library (hereafter cited as Mitchell fonds, University of Calgary).

school's entry in the 1966 Eastern Ontario One-Act Drama Festival, where it won the awards for best overall play, high school play, director, and actor. Ten years later, spurred on by the success of his stage play *Back to Beulah* (which won the 1976 Chalmers Canadian Play Award), Mitchell began adapting *The Black Bonspiel of Wullie MacCrimmon* to a full-length stage play. The first two professional stage productions were done by the Peterborough Festival of Canadian Theatre (1977) and Theatre Calgary (1979). Both were directed by Guy Sprung and starred Hugh Webster as Wullie. The Theatre Calgary production was a major hit and its run was extended a week. It was so successful—over 16,000 tickets were sold—that Theatre Calgary mounted a new production the following season which sold another 12,000 tickets. In the next three years Lennoxville Festival, Magnus Theatre (Thunder Bay), Manitoba Theatre Centre (Winnipeg), Vancouver Playhouse, and Citadel Theatre (Edmonton) mounted very successful productions. To date there have been about seventy productions of *The Black Bonspiel*, and it has been seen by over a quarter of a million theatre-goers. It has been a budget saver for many theatres, frequently filling theatres to over 90 percent capacity.[3]

Mitchell's depiction of the Devil as a travelling salesman who deals "in Wholesale Souls and Retail Sin" sets the tone for a light-hearted version of the traditional Faust legend. Wullie MacCrimmon,

---

[3]Manitoba Theatre Company's production drew houses of 92 percent capacity (the best-selling play in MTC's history to date) and grossed $182,000. The Citadel production sold 21,300 tickets (97 percent total house capacity). In an article on the Blyth Festival's production, Jamie Portman wrote, "W.O. Mitchell has never been done on Blyth, but his *Black Bonspiel of Wullie MacCrimmon*—which joined the repertory last week—has been a big money maker for any theatre that has presented it" ("Blyth Festival Back on Firm Footing," *Ottawa Citizen*, August 10, 1994). H.J. Kirchoff wrote, "The stage version has sold out nearly everywhere it's been staged, and the all-Canadian Blyth Festival—anxious to get people back into the seats after two or three bad years—chose to revive it...." ("Bonspiel a Good Match for Blyth," *Globe and Mail*, August 9, 1994, C.3). Martin Morrow commented in the *Calgary Herald* on Theatre Calgary's 1988 production: "The show, a revival of the most popular play in TC's 20-year history, sold out in the two scheduled weeks of its run in the Max Bell Theatre and was held over an additional week." It was the "most successful show for the struggling company so far this season" ("The Devil and the Black Bonspiel," *Calgary Herald*, November 25, 1988).

a shoemaker in a small Alberta foothills town, is tempted by the Devil to trade his soul for a victory in the MacDonald Brier, the Canadian national curling championships (currently called the Tim Horton's Brier). Wullie is no great sinner, just "a dawd here, a dawd there," but in a moment of dreamy self-indulgence he says, "I would give anything... (*Low and reverent*) utterly anything for to skip the winning rink in the Macdonald Brier Finals." In a flash, the Devil appears saying, "That's a bargain, Wullie MacCrimmon." The Devil is interested in Wullie not only because winning Wullie's devout continuing Presbyterian soul will help settle his score with God, but also because he has a dream. For millennia he has been a loser, but with Wullie playing third on his curling team from Hell, he hopes to finally beat God's team in the Celestial Brier. After some haggling, Wullie signs a revised version of the Devil's "standard soul-for-fair-recompense contract": Wullie will curl a match against the Devil, and if the Devil wins, Wullie is bound to curl third for him in Hell. But if Wullie wins, the Devil will grant him his wish to win the MacDonald Brier and Wullie will not lose his soul.

Mitchell's story about Wullie's curling duel with the Devil stands in a long tradition of Christian folktales about individuals who make deals with the Devil. His idea to write a story in this tradition may have been triggered by Stephen Vincent Benét's short story and one-act stage play, "The Devil and Daniel Webster."[4] Some years after Mitchell wrote his short story, he played the role of Mr. Scratch (the Devil) in Benét's play when it was produced by the Fort Qu'Appelle Drama Workshop in the summer of 1953. Another significant influence behind *The Black Bonspiel* is the North American tall-tale tradition. Mitchell's first success as a writer came with his "Jake and the Kid" stories,[5] in which Jake Trumper, the hired hand, is an inveterate tall-tale teller, or liar. He tells the kid how he invented the buffalo

---

[4]Benét's story, published in 1937, won an O. Henry Award for Best American Short Stories in 1938. It was inspired by Washington Irving's "The Devil and Tom Walker" (1824).

[5]The Jake and the Kid stories first appeared in *Maclean's* in the 1940s, then became one of CBC's most popular weekly radio series from 1950 to 1956. A collection of thirteen of these stories, *Jake and the Kid*, was published by Macmillan of Canada in 1961.

jumping pound, "drunk Catawba wine with Sir John A," and "made Looie Riel say uncle three times—once in English, once in Cree, and the third time in French."[6] One of these stories, "The Liar Hunter," is specifically about the rationale of tall-tale telling. Godfrey, an anthropologist from the east, describes the existentialist impulse that lies behind western tall-tale liars:

> This is a hard country, I don't have to tell you that. There are— drouth, blizzards, loneliness. A man's a pretty small thing out on all this prairie. He is at the mercy of the elements.... These men lie about the things that hurt them most. Their yarns are about the winters and how cold they are, the summers and how dry they are. In this country you get the deepest snow, the worst dust storms, the biggest hail-stones.... Rust and dust and hail and sawfly and cutworm and drouth are terrible things, but not half as frightening if they are made ridiculous. If a man can laugh at them he's won half the battle. When he exaggerates things he isn't lying really; it's a defence, the defence of exaggeration. He can either do that or squeal.... People in this country aren't squealers.[7]

The Black Bonspiel of Wullie MacCrimmon is an elaborate tall tale in which a foothills-town cobbler challenges the Devil himself to a curling match—and wins.

Wullie, like Uncle Sean in *Who Has Seen the Wind*, Jake in *Jake and the Kid*, Daddy Sherry in *The Kite*, Archie Nicotine in *The Vanishing Point* and *Since Daisy Creek*, and King Motherwell in *How I Spent My Summer Holidays*, grew out of Mitchell's essentially existentialist vision. These characters have done battle with tough times and, despite seemingly unbeatable odds, they are "yea-sayers" who persist and live their lives according to a code of honour which often outrages conventional society's sense of propriety and morality. Uncle Sean rages profanely against his neighbours (such as Bent

---

[6]Mitchell, *Jake and the Kid*, 184.
[7]*Jake and the Kid*, 105.

Candy, a clean-mouthed Baptist elder whose soul is as black as his drifting topsoil). Candy's farming methods turn a quick dollar but destroy the soil and exacerbate the effects of the drought,[8] whereas Uncle Sean's visionary farming methods create a garden despite the drought. Daddy Sherry is the oldest man in the world, and throughout his life his motto has been, "never settle for less." He lives his life with grace and daring and advises, "Live loose an' soople an' you'll come through without a scratch. Live careful an' you'll break your goddam neck."[9] Wullie stubbornly refuses to join Reverend Pringle's United Church, for he is an old-style Protestant, a latter-day Martin Luther, who insists, "Here I stand!" Reverend Pringle is a sympathetic character whose more modern religious concept of an inner psychological Hell and Heaven runs into stiff opposition from Wullie who believes in a literal Hell, "a three-dimensional, crackling, actually burnin' hell.... Where we may roast in blazing fire from everlasting to everlasting." We are fascinated by Wullie because he dares to go head-to-head with the Devil himself. At the end of the first act, after he has signed his contract with the Devil and made preparations for the match with his team members, Wullie raises a large cup of scotch to the audience and invokes the clan Grant's rallying battle cry, "Stand fast, Craigellachie. And—curl to beat Hell."

Wullie, like Uncle Sean in *Who Has Seen the Wind* and King in *How I Spent My Summer Holidays*, has no patience with sanctimonious morality which unthinkingly paints the world with broad brushstrokes of good and evil, and which in a busy-body way attempts—with various commandments—to control how people live their lives. King argues that "there has been too much thou-shalt-notting" in the world which boils down to one commandment, "Thou shalt not have fun."[10] *The Black Bonspiel*'s Annie Brown is a character who crystallizes this mentality with her gossiping ways about what she perceives as immoral behaviour (curling on Sundays) and books (reading Shakespeare and Chaucer). Book-banning Annie

---

[8]Mitchell, *Who Has Seen the Wind*, 21–22.
[9]Mitchell, stage play version of *The Kite* in *Dramatic W.O. Mitchell*, 156.
[10]Mitchell, *How I Spent My Summer Holidays*, 31–32.

is a new character Mitchell added when he expanded the television play into the full-length stage play.[11] Her creation was influenced by a spate of censorship incidents across Canada at that time. The Pentecostal Assemblies of Canada urged banning a number of books from school lists, including *Who Has Seen the Wind*.[12] The Reverend Ken Campbell and his Renaissance Canada lobby group also went after *Who Has Seen the Wind*, as well as books by Alice Munro and Margaret Laurence. On one occasion Mitchell was involved in a lively debate with Campbell about the issue of banning books from schools. He recalled that, after the show, Campbell approached him, all friendly and with a big smile: "Bill, I bear you no animus." Mitchell, refusing to shake his hand, said, "Well Reverend, I don't bear you any animus either—but my animosity towards you has no bounds."[13] Mitchell took every opportunity he could to attack publicly the book banners, and he used Annie Brown as part of this attack. Perhaps Mitchell's animosity surfaces too obviously in Annie Brown and he sacrificed character depth for satirical caricature. Guy Sprung writes, "It was uncomfortable watching the actresses who had to play Annie Brown going through the agony of trying to give reality to that thinnest of roles."[14]

Mitchell conceived of the writer and his audience as "creative partners" in the art experience of reading or theatre-going—both share in the creation of a compelling story illusion. He also saw his role as playwright in terms of a creative collaboration with the director, actors, and stage and light designers, and *The Black Bonspiel* leaves some rich and challenging space for his theatre collaborators to play with. For instance, Mitchell's stories often satirize town and city rivalries and their penchant for stereotyping other communities as Sodoms and Gomorrahs, or dens of iniquity. Although the play is set in the Alberta foothills town of Wildrose, not far from Calgary,

---

[11] In the television play she is called Mrs. Button and has only two short speeches in the opening scene.
[12] "Pentecostals Seek Ban of Books from Schools," *The Albertan*, August 30, 1978.
[13] Barbara and Ormond Mitchell, *Mitchell: The Life of W.O. Mitchell*, 297.
[14] Sprung, "Acting W.O.," 315.

Mitchell invited directors to substitute other place names in various speeches in the play so that each production had a local appeal. In the Peterborough production, audiences were delighted when Annie Brown guesses that the mysterious dark stranger must be a travelling man from Toronto, and later when the Devil says "Toronto is always rich and rewarding territory" for his business in retail souls and sin.

Directors also added local connotations to the portrayal of the Devil. Guy Sprung planned to cast Jean Archambault as the Devil for the Lennoxville Festival because he was "the spitting image of René Levesque," a separatist whom anglophone Quebecers saw as a devil.[15] In one of the Theatre Calgary productions, the Devil did a Peter Lougheed[16] impersonation in his "let those upper bastards freeze in the dark" speech, and in the Grand Theatre production's prompt script the Devil is directed to impersonate Richard Nixon in the scene where he says, "Now—I want to make this thing perfectly clear." The members of the Devil's curling team were changed in some productions. Alberta Theatre Projects and Grand Theatre replaced Guy Fawkes with Lizzy Borden, the notorious American spinster who murdered her father and stepmother with a hatchet. It was felt audiences would not know who Guy Fawkes was, and substituting him with Borden added another female role to the play. She appeared with a hatchet attached to her curling broom. In the Citadel Theatre production, both Judas Iscariot and Guy Fawkes were replaced. Joe Schoctor, the founder of Citadel Theatre, felt the Judas Iscariot character would offend Jewish audience members. Mitchell initially resisted these changes (arguing that Judas is simply a "lapsed Christian"), but relented and agreed to write lines for Nero to replace Judas. Guy Fawkes was replaced by a character called Murphy.[17]

---

[15]Sprung, 314.

[16]Lougheed was the premier of Alberta who, in the early 1980s, fought against Pierre Trudeau's National Energy Program.

[17]The actors we contacted who played in this production, including Richard Gishler who played Murphy, could not remember who Murphy was supposed to be. Gishler felt that the Murphy replacement weakened the play and regretted not being able to play the original Guy Fawkes.

There are a number of staging challenges in *The Black Bonspiel*. It calls for some exciting pyrotechnics in the entrances and exits of the Devil and his team, but a number of productions expanded on these and devised other elaborate special effects. In some productions the Devil's tail had a mechanism and flash-pot in it so that when it dropped out of his coat in the opening scene, it flashed fire. The smoke wisping out of the Devil's shoes on Wullie's shoes-to-be-repaired shelf (red smoke in some productions) was a tricky effect to achieve because of down-drafts in some theatres. Special gloves were designed for the Devil so that he appeared to light his cigar and Pipe's cigarette with a flame from the end of his finger, and in one production the Devil wore a cannon flame shooter inside his sleeve. In the Lennoxville and the Manitoba Theatre Centre productions the Devil had a broom which shot "large jets of flame" at his team making them disappear "in 3 simultaneous explosions of smoke and flame."[18]

The Devil's disappearance in a "huge cloud of smoke and flame accompanied by a lambasting blast of thunder" at the end of Act 1, his rink's appearance in a "loud explosion, flash of lightning" at the beginning of Act 2, and their disappearance in a "lambasting explosion of sound and lightning and smoke" at the end of Act 2, were often done through the stage floor using fog, smoke, lights, and sound effects. In the Manitoba Theatre Centre production, photo flashes on a beam and flashing lights were directed at the audience's eyes to momentarily blind them so that when their eyes adjusted, the Devil and his team seemed to appear and disappear out of thin air. They also used both mineral-oil smoke and carbon dioxide (dry ice) so that the smoke would both rise and drift.[19] On occasion these special effects caused some problems. An Alberta Theatre Projects performance report said that "smoke from devil disappearance is overwhelming audience—have asked Adrian to cut back slightly on

---

[18]"Special Effects," September 30, 1981, P4438, file 22, Manitoba Theatre Centre Archives, Archives of Manitoba.

[19]Production Notes, December 14, 1981, P4438, file 22, Manitoba Theatre Centre Archives, Archives of Manitoba.

powder (my kingdom for exhaust fans)."[20] One of the Citadel Theatre reports described a near accident: "during the Devil's final disappearance at the end of act 2 there were flying sparks from the telegraph pole flashpot, d.s. flashpot, and the u.s. flashpot, where Mr. Bede [Devil] stands. These may have been flaring chunks of magnesium. No-one was hurt, and the overall effect was quite spectacular!"[21] In their 1993 production, Theatre Aquarius used a mixture of "Smokeless Shotgun Powder" and liquid "Red Flame Additive" for the explosive flames in which the Devil and his team appear and disappear, and a "'Rosco Fog/Smoke Fluid' for the fog machines." [22] Each show used sixty pounds of dry ice and their budget for the pyrotechnic and fog effects was over $6,500.[23]

The biggest staging challenge for this play is Wullie's curling battle with the Devil in the second act. The 1966 Lakefield College production did not use curling rocks, relying instead on mime and sound effects to create the illusion of the bonspiel. Against taped sounds of the rumble of granite on ice, the whacking of brooms, and the crack of rocks colliding in the house (all recorded at the local curling rink), the actors mimicked throwing and sweeping imaginary rocks. But most professional productions stage the bonspiel so that the audience sees curling rocks coming from offstage and into a curling rink house in full view. Elaborate techniques were used to create a surface which looked like ice and on which the rocks would slide as if on real ice. Most productions used actual forty-four pound granite curling rocks, so the surface had to be durable. Theatre Calgary used sheets of three-quarter inch plywood framed with an additional two inches of ply which was then covered with "arena board" (material used on the boards in hockey rinks) coated with silicone. They also used a water and liquid silicone mix in a watering can which Pipe periodically

[20]Performance Report for 1997 production of *The Black Bonspiel of Wullie MacCrimmon* files, Alberta Theatre Projects Archives, Alberta Theatre Projects Office.

[21]Performance Report, November 16, 1982, PR1985.0376, Box 3, file 43, Citadel Theatre Archives, Provincial Archives of Alberta.

[22]Stewart Brown, "FX," *Hamilton Spectator*, November 9, 1993.

[23]Technical Notes, MC A942116, file 4, Theatre Aquarius Archives, Archival and Special Collections, University of Guelph.

sprinkled on the surface, supposedly to "pebble"[24] the "ice," but in fact to keep the arena board slick. Manitoba Theatre Centre used "battleship linoleum (known for its sturdiness) for the surface" and treated it with "varathanes and liquid silicone."[25]

   In the first Theatre Calgary productions, Pat Flood arranged snow banks and a fence to hide the actual results of curled rocks so that the curlers did not have to make precise shots.[26] Subsequent professional productions, which left the house in full view, prepared their actors for their curling roles with coaching from expert curlers at the local curling rinks, and frequently crucial rocks were thrown from offstage by the experts to make sure the winning rocks were actually winning rocks. The actors could not take the blasé attitude Mitchell took in his curling experiences in the early 1940s. He was notorious in Castor for his "devil-may-care" attitude as he "sloshed around" in unbuckled overshoes. At one bonspiel, a buckle fell off his overshoe and stopped a rock so that it had to be taken out of play, and when his team was conferring about the next shot, Mitchell said, "why don't we just throw a rock into the middle of that mess and see what happens?"[27] *The Black Bonspiel* actors have to make accurate shots on cue, especially in the last end, so stage managers devised elaborate blocking charts for each series of curled rocks. The last series in the Alberta Theatre Projects' charts is headed in bold caps, "THESE SHOTS MUST BE MADE!"[28] But sometimes it was necessary for what the Alberta Theatre Projects stage manager called the "miracle," whereby one of the actors surreptitiously nudged a rock closer to the button.[29] On one occasion the cast had to create some impromptu confusion to hide the fact that the stage manager had curled a rock

---

[24]Curling term: to sprinkle the ice with water droplets before a match begins. The droplets freeze into small "pebbles," which enhance the curling motion of the rocks.

[25]Dennis Kucherawy, "Devil Slides Out," *Winnipeg Free Press*, December 30, 1981.

[26]Eric Dawson, "Behind the Scenes," *Calgary Herald*, circa March 5, 1979.

[27]Barbara and Ormond Mitchell, *W.O.: The Life of W.O. Mitchell*, 269.

[28]Production Notes, 1997, *Black Bonspiel of Wullie MacCrimmon* files. Alberta Theatre Projects Archives, Alberta Theatre Projects Office.

[29]The Grand Theatre called it the "God cue": "God came into play when Wullie's last rock came up short by about 6 inches." Performance Report, February 27, 2005, Grand Theatre Archives, Archival and Special Collections, University of Guelph.

from offstage which was so good it made the Devil's team the winners. The Citadel Theatre production avoided this problem by having the Devil curl both of his last rocks "up against the side of the rink to ensure that the good guys win. This looks better than the accidental 'cheating.'"[30] Western Canada Theatre Company's production at the Sagebrush Theatre added a new character to the play, Angel (played by a grade six student wearing wings). When a curling rock went astray, she cued the cast to freeze and then slid the rock into its proper position. There were other hazards in the curling match with which the actors had to contend, such as tripping over rocks or slipping. In one of the Citadel shows, Malleable (played by Wally McSween), "slipped during his curl—he didn't hurt himself but split his trousers in the crotch." However, "the hell entrance was applauded by an appreciative audience, and aside from Wally's mishap, the show went smoothly!"[31]

Many productions had great success with their pyrotechnics and their creation of a realistic illusion of a close curling match with Wully's soul hanging in the balance. Audiences in particular applauded the sudden and explosive entrances of the Devil and his rink. They also cheered the good curling shots which put Wullie's team in a winning position. On the Grand Theatre's closing night, "The curling match was fantastic as the good guys won fair and square—which pleased the 150 curlers in the audience." Bill Carr, who played Pipe in the Neptune Theatre Production, recalled that "the audience was on every rock and seemed mesmerized—there was no suspension of disbelief—just raw visceral belief and joy."[32] Probably the best compliment paid to a successful staging of *The Black Bonspiel*'s curling came in one of the shows in Theatre Calgary's 1980 production. The Canadian Brier was being hosted by

---

[30]Performance Report, October 31, 1982, PR1985.0376, Box 3, file 43, Citadel Theatre Archives, Provincial Archives of Alberta.

[31]Performance Report, November 20, 1982, PR1985.0376, Box 3, file 43, Citadel Theatre Archives, Provincial Archives of Alberta.

[32]Bill Carr, email message to author, December 10, 2008.

Calgary, and the organizers bought out one of the evening's perform-ances. As Guy Sprung recalls, "playing to an audience of curling aficionados was one of those rare magical evenings of theatre."[33] The play obviously left quite an impression. In one of the Brier games following this show, some of the curlers "went out and swept backwards on one shot."[34]

⇒•◦•⇐

THE DEVIL'S INSTRUMENT

The Devil's Instrument and *The Black Bonspiel of Wullie MacCrimmon* approach religion, hell, damnation, and the Devil from different angles. In *The Black Bonspiel of Wullie MacCrimmon* there is little to admire about the Devil—except his sardonic sense of humour. He is closer to the devil tricksters of medieval legend and to Christopher Marlowe's devils in *Dr. Faustus*. A bully and a cheat, the audience cheers when Wullie meets him head-on and beats him at his own game. In *The Devil's Instrument*, however, Mitchell follows the Romantics' vision of the Devil as a positive Promethean figure who, as representative of creative and sexual energy, fosters freedom against the limiting forces of a puritanical and materialistic society. Darius, a stranger in town, tempts Jacob away from the colony, an imprisoning Garden of Eden, by giving him a musical instrument which unlocks Jacob's innate musical talent. Jacob leaves the colony in the final scene. Like Adam and Eve at the end of Milton's *Paradise Lost* when they are evicted from Eden, Jacob has all "the world...before" him as he takes his "solitary way." He also has the freedom to choose his "place of rest," but Marta, Jacob's Eve, does not come with him.[35]

The idea for "The Devil's Instrument" began with an encounter Mitchell had with two Hutterite boys in New Dayton, Alberta in

[33]Sprung, "Acting W.O.," 314.

[34]Dennis Kucherawy, "Devil Slides Out," *Winnipeg Free Press*, December 30, 1981.

[35]Milton, *Paradise Lost*, 12.646–49.

1943. The boys were looking at a mouth organ in the glass counter display of Tom's Café:

> I said, "Pretty nice mouth organ, hey?" and they agreed it was. "I guess you'd like to have one of those." Each of them said no, he wouldn't. I said, "Why not?" They said, "It's the Devil's instrument—you would risk your immortal soul." I was fascinated. "What would be wrong with blowing through a mouth organ?" They said, "Well, it says in the Bible you've got to love the Lord your God with all your heart and all your soul. If you had that mouth organ you might love blowing that mouth organ too much. It would be wicked because it would diminish your love for God." It was interesting to me—I hadn't thought of love as a diminishable or exhaustible quantity. These guys had, or had been told so. I said, "Well, that means you mustn't love anything except God." They said, "Yeah, that's right." I said, "Well, a girl? Your wife? If you loved her you would diminish, take away from the quantity of love you had for God." They said, "Yes."[36]

Intrigued by this exchange and what he had learned about the Hutterites in New Dayton, Mitchell wrote a short story called "Peter and the Goose Boss."

When Mitchell moved to High River in 1944, he learned a great deal more about Hutterite communal life in the two colonies nearby. Hutterites were a familiar sight in High River. The men dressed in black trousers, shirts, and suspenders, with a black felt hat; the women dressed in long black dresses with an apron, lace-up boots, and a polka-dot kerchief covering their heads. When Mitchell went out to fly-fish along Willow Creek, he would visit with families at the Macmillan Colony. He was attracted to "these people of the gentle persuasion," by the way their strict religious beliefs were an integral part of their day-to-day life, and by their dogged commitment to a communal life. They had suffered religious persecution for over five centuries in half a dozen countries before ending up in Canada in

---

[36]Barbara and Ormond Mitchell, *W.O.: The Life of W.O. Mitchell*, 297.

1918. Over the next twenty years, the Alberta community grew suspicious of the Hutterites' success and their accumulation of land, a suspicion which increased when World War II broke out and the Hutterites, who are pacifists, refused to serve. In 1942, Alberta's Social Credit government banned all land sales to Hutterites. Following the war, it brought in more legislation, culminating in the Communal Properties Act of 1955, which restricted the amount and location of Hutterite land purchases. Throughout the 1950s and 1960s, Mitchell was a champion of the Hutterites' rights, writing a number of articles, radio shows, and television documentaries exposing how they were being persecuted by Albertans.[37] Mitchell's creative imagination was often attracted to ethnic minorities under attack (see, for example, the Stoney Indians in *The Vanishing Point* and the Chinese in *Who Has Seen the Wind*), and many of his stories explore the paradoxical and complex tensions of a love-hate triangle: an ethnic minority, the larger majority demanding assimilation, and the individual caught between the two.

Mitchell was also bothered by some aspects of Hutterite colony life. He sensed that it was characterized by a deep-seated materialism which, paradoxically, co-existed with its Puritanism,[38] both of which were inimical to artistic expression. Their desire for a simple, spiritual life forbade their members from participating in the outside world's lifestyle with its rights of private ownership, politics, and educational and legal institutions. They saw the arts (music, books, radio, theatre, and movies) as the Devil's tools for tempting sinners away from a life of useful work devoted to God. However, unlike other religious

---

[37]For example, "No Man Is," a drama for CBC's *Summer Fallow* broadcast on May 29, 1961, showed the positive value of the Hutterite people and their colonies, as did "The People Who Don't Want Equality," *Macleans*, July 3, 1965: 9. Mitchell wrote a satiric letter to Mr. Ernest Manning, Premier of Alberta, attacking his government's treatment of the Hutterites, in particular Mr. Hooke's (one of his cabinet ministers) comment that relaxing the Communal Properties Act to allow Hutterites to buy land "would be like letting a pack of starving dogs off their leashes" (for whole letter see *An Evening with W.O. Mitchell*, 221–22).

[38]The root of this paradox may lie in the Calvinist belief that material wealth is a sign that one belongs to the Elect, God's chosen.

communal groups such as the Amish and Mennonites who rejected all modern technology, many of the Hutterite colonies embraced new advances in agricultural methods and equipment which increased their affluence.[39]

Mitchell was opposed to any authority which repressively moved into another individual's or minority's territory. On the one hand, he was outraged by the bigotry of the Alberta Social Credit government's legislation, which infringed on the rights of the Hutterites; on the other hand, he was critical of the power the colonies held over their own individual members. The Bosses controlled every aspect of Hutterite life, including when and to whom young people were married. This control, and its impact on the emotional and creative life of the individual, became the focus of "The Devil's Instrument." Using first-hand observation of Macmillan colony life, Mitchell began expanding "Peter and the Goose Boss" into a 15,000 word novella in which fifteen-year-old Jacob Schunk rebels against the colony Bosses. "The Devil's Instrument," completed in 1947, explores Hutterite repression of its own members, particularly of a potentially creative adolescent who is denied the opportunity to fully explore and express his emotional, intellectual, and artistic identity.

In the novella's opening scene in the Nu-Way Café, a stranger buys Jacob the mouth organ he has been admiring in the display case. Although he has been taught that the practice of any art and the pleasure it gives are sinful, Jacob cannot help himself: "He played it, a youth in a dream, in a trance, exalted and enchanted by the magic of its sound." At the same time, Jacob falls in love with Marta, and Mitchell links his awakening artistic and sexual passions. Though forbidden to meet until they are paired for marriage, Jacob and Marta meet clandestinely behind one of the haystacks. Whenever Jacob thinks of Marta, he feels "a slight quickening of his heart and a breathlessness equalled only when he contemplated playing his mouth organ." For a while he gives up his mouth organ, and buries it in the straw stack.

---

[39]On a per capita/land basis Hutterites were, and have remained, the prairie provinces' most productive farmers. See Ryan, "Hutterites."

In town, he again meets the stranger who reveals that he is Jacob's brother, Darius, who had been excommunicated years before for defying the Bosses. Darius tries to persuade Jacob to leave the colony, arguing that Jacob is not free, that "there are no Hutterite poets, for the colony kills what is beautiful," and that the Devil is "Boss over all the Bosses!"' Jacob does not leave with Darius, but he cannot resist either Marta or his mouth organ. He is discovered, his mouth organ is smashed on the blacksmith's anvil, and Jacob and Marta are sentenced to shunning (Jacob for three months, Marta for one month). The Bosses also decree that Jacob will not marry Marta. When he tries to speak to her, Marta runs from him. Jacob also flees, but away from the colony to find his brother who "would give him another mouth organ."[40]

Jacob's self-exile from the colony is an ambivalent victory. Those forces in the Hutterite colony that are inimical to his creative spirit and the fulfilment of his identity are also present, in more subtle and insidious forms, in the larger colony of the outside society. This is hinted at in Darius's response when Jacob asks him if he is happy: "Happiness is not everything. I must be honest with you. I am free. Anyway—I am free."[41] In the novella version of "The Devil's Instrument," Darius says,

> 'I must be honest with you. I am free—"If I forgot thee, O Jerusalem"'—his voice died away. 'Anyway, I am free,' he said again.[42]

---

[40]Above quotations are taken from the 1947 manuscript of "The Devil's Instrument," Mitchell fonds, University of Calgary, MsC19.19.23. Macmillan of Canada and Little Brown (US) were about to publish "The Devil's Instrument" in 1949 when it was discovered that another book, *The Dream Gate*, had just been published, which had exactly the same plot (a Hutterite boy who gets into trouble for playing a mouth organ). It was thought that the writer had heard the radio version of "The Devil's Instrument" and had freely borrowed from it. Plagiarism charges were considered, but in the end it was decided to simply postpone publishing the novella for a few years. It never has been published in its original novella form.

[41]Mitchell, *The Devil's Instrument, Dramatic W.O. Mitchell*, 27.

[42]1949 manuscript, Mitchell fonds, University of Calgary, MsC19.19.23.

In this reference to Psalm 137, Darius compares himself to the Israelites who, exiled to Babylon, mourn for Jerusalem and Zion. Although he is "free," the exiled Darius still has a deep nostalgia for his Hutterite community. He has gained his freedom at a dear price, the love and safety of a caring family and community.

Jacob's situation is universal. He is a Hutterite version of James Joyce's Stephen Daedalus, and Mitchell's novella is a portrait of the musician/artist as a young man whose first stirrings of sexual and artistic energies are thwarted by his puritan and materialistic society. Jacob's final rebellion and self-exile are not as self-conscious as those of Stephen, but he too finally rebels and escapes from his imprisoning island, flies by the nets of religion, materialism, and a powerful hierarchical society which tries to predetermine and control every aspect of his life. Mitchell uses the Hutterite society's repression of creative energy in its young as an exaggerated reflection of the larger puritan and materialistic society's repression of the young, a theme he explores in many of his works.[43] For example, Carlyle in *The Vanishing Point* and Hugh in *How I Spent my Summer Holidays* go through a series of memory flashbacks to their childhood and adolescent years as they come to terms with the emotional and psychological damage of their puritan upbringing. Old Kacky, the strap-wielding Presbyterian teacher who appears in both of these novels, plays the same repressive role in Carlyle's and Hugh's education that the Bosses play in Jacob's life.[44]

The staging challenges of *The Devil's Instrument* are very different from those of *The Black Bonspiel of Wullie MacCrimmon*. It is probably because of these challenges, as well as the large number of roles (twenty-one with few that can be doubled up), that this play has

---

[43]In the program for the Alberta Theatre Projects production, Mitchell says, "*The Devil's Instrument* is not intended as an exotic little regional story. At one time, I actually thought I would not make reference to Hutterites—I would just let it be understood that Jacob's community was a rather novel, fundamentalist and religious communal society. But as it stands, the play is an illustration of the struggle that any artist has in what is necessarily an inartistic and disapproving society." W.O. Mitchell, "The Author's View," Program for the Alberta Theatre Projects' performance of *The Devil's Instrument* (1977): 6.

[44]See also Brian's teacher, Miss MacDonald, in *Who Has Seen the Wind*.

only been given two full stage productions. While *The Black Bonspiel*'s actors had to develop some curling skills, shots that went astray could be camouflaged. Ideally, the actor who plays Jacob should be an accomplished harmonica player who can make all of his musical shots, and the play should have an orchestral soundscape to complement the harmonica solos. The music in this play not only creates atmosphere and serves as a transitional element between scenes, it is central to the play's theme and emotional impact. Jacob plays a wide range of music on his "little mouth organ"—from Gregorian hymnal, to folk and country ballad, to coyote "howls" and train "whoops," to finally what Jacob describes as "tunes that have never been played before."[45] When the Oats and Barley boss pronounces at Jacob's trial that John the Blacksmith will place Jacob's mouth organ on his anvil, "and he shall smash it," the impact should be as powerful as a death. Miles McNamara, who played Jacob in Ron Hartman's Ontario Youtheatre production of *The Devil's Instrument* at Peterborough Theatre Guild, was up to the task. He gave a deeply moving portrayal of a young man torn apart with his love for music, for Marta, and for God.

This play's dramatic origins in radio and television result in a stage play of twenty-six scenes (some of them very short) with rapid transitions from one locale to another (interior of Wong's café, to exterior of Jacob and Peter in the buggy, to the exterior well-witching scene at the Hutterite colony, to interior colony sleeping quarters, to a montage of scenes showing the colony coming alive in the morning, and so on). The director and stage manager have to be inventive with their use of music, lighting, blackouts, and multiple stage areas with minimal props (which indicate where a scene is taking place) in order to maintain a seamless flow to the action. Douglas Riske, director of the Alberta Theatre Projects production, wanted "to try to keep the cinematic quality of the script with scenes flowing one to another,

---

[45]The novella describes Jacob, as he plays his mouth organ, as "a youth in a dream, in a trance, exalted and enchanted by the magic of its sound. It was not a Hutterite tune he played[;] it was not cowboy music; it was no song that he had ever listened to; it had never been played before. It was beautiful." Mitchell fonds, University of Calgary, MsC19.19.23.

even at times almost overlapping,"[46] and Pat Flood "transformed the tiny stage into a visually exciting world which contains a small-town café, the rooms of various homes and barns, as well as fields and roadways."[47] The ATP production had a very small budget, and Riske dealt with the large cast problem by using only six actors and a number of life-size puppets to create the illusion of a larger community. Some of the puppets were at times manipulated by the other actors. Riske's use of puppets works on a symbolic level as well, for the image of people as puppets on strings being controlled by a puppeteer reflects the community members being controlled by the Bosses. They also emphasized the stylistic treatment which this play invites—it is not as realistic or naturalistic a play as *The Black Bonspiel* and other Mitchell plays, and some of the stark scenes highlighted with the black and white Hutterite costumes, especially Jacob's judgement scene, push this play into allegory. It is a kind of modern medieval morality play in which Jacob is an Everyman whose creative soul is beset by various temptations and restrictions.

Mitchell's original plan had been to publish *The Black Bonspiel of Wullie MacCrimmon* and *The Devil's Instrument* in a Devil trilogy under the title, "The Devil is a Travelling Man." In the fall of 1951, he had mapped out a rough narrative for the third story "in which Satan takes a holiday up the Highwood River."[48] The main character, in his mid-forties, lives in a town on the lower reaches of the Highwood, and he too is faced with an existentialist dilemma. All his life he has had a passion for fly-fishing, and because he has just been diagnosed with terminal cancer, he knows this will be his last season. Over the years he has had unsuccessful skirmishes with a particularly large brown trout that haunts a series of pools in the Highwood. One afternoon, a stranger appears on the river. To the disgust of the fly fisherman, the stranger seems to be having some success with his spinning hardware and bait. The stranger approaches and watches as

---

[46]Douglas Riske to W.O. Mitchell, 8 August 1977. Alberta Theatre Projects Archives, Alberta Theatre Office.

[47]Louis Hobson, "Mini-Mitchell," *The Albertan*, September 27, 1977.

[48]Barbara and Ormond Mitchell, *Mitchell: The Life of W.O. Mitchell*, 38.

the fisherman casts his dry fly over and over, receiving no strikes. He then offers the fisherman one of his lures, assuring him that it will change his luck. The fisherman declines, saying he only fishes with flies. The stranger persists, offering him a salted minnow and telling him that if he casts it in a particular place in the pool he will hook the largest brown trout that has ever come out of the Highwood, a fish so large it will hold the North American record for years to come. Mitchell played with various endings to this story, one of which was the fisherman refusing to compromise and continuing to cast his fly as the stranger leaves and the evening darkness closes down on the river.

Mitchell never developed this story idea of the Devil as a fisherman of souls any further. But we are left with two of the planned trilogy, and these two plays do make a nice complementary pair. One play invites realistic staging and elaborate pyrotechnical special effects, the other an allegorical and minimalist treatment with a strong musical score. One play places the Devil as an actual character—not what Wullie calls a "wishy-washy symbolical" Devil—in the realistic setting of a 1930s small-town curling match. It is from the incongruity of this mix that the play gains much of its humour. The other play creates a more stylistic setting in a Hutterite community in which the Devil is symbolically implicit in Jacob's brother, Darius, who tempts Jacob not with an apple, but with a mouth organ. One play on the surface is simply a comic fable, or tall tale, but has a serious existentialist vision and some criticism of puritan small-town Canada underlying it. The other, apart from a few comic scenes, is a more sombre and complex examination of the individual's thwarted desire to express and fulfill his artistic and emotional freedom—it verges on tragedy and evokes a much deeper emotional impact. Sixty years after these two stories were first conceived, they continue to be relevant. The Devil has a steady supply of potential players for his rink from Hell, and the arts continue to be threatened by materialism and, in our politically correct times, by new forms of puritanical "Thou shalt nots."

NOTE ON THE TEXT

In 1982, Macmillan of Canada published five of Mitchell's stage plays under the title *Dramatic W.O. Mitchell*. We have used Macmillan's edition for the texts of *The Black Bonspiel of Wullie MacCrimmon* and *The Devil's Instrument*, including the introduction for each play that Mitchell wrote for this collection of plays. In the footnotes we have added supplementary material from earlier versions and from the prompt scripts of some of the productions.

THE BLACK BONSPIEL
OF WULLIE MacCRIMMON

INTRODUCTION BY W.O. MITCHELL

The Black Mass, probably deriving from Zoroastrianism[1] with its co-equal and eternal principles of Good and Evil, was practised by worshippers of Satan. A travesty of the Christian mass,[2] this ritual of impiety did all things in reverse, reaching its peak in France in the nineteenth century and not surprisingly among writers, who have traditionally belonged to the immoral minority.

Less well known is the Black Bonspiel, a diabolically backward celebration of the sport of curling. Until recent times, except in Scotland and in Canada, rink and rock and broom have won few fervent converts. There were many black bonspiels curled during the Wars of the Covenanters[3] in the seventeenth century to celebrate the powers of darkness in Scotland. Had the Irish embraced curling, no

---

[1] A dualistic religion based on a conflict between light and darkness (founded by Avestan Zarathustra in Persia in the sixth century BCE).
[2] Eucharist, Christian sacrament.
[3] The Covenanters formed a religious (Presbyterian) and political movement in Scotland which led to wars in Scotland, England, and Ireland.

doubt black bonspiels would be as popular as ambush and bombing are there today. The Reverend Ian Paisley[4] could be calling down the wrath of his Protestant God upon Sabbath[5] curlers risking their immortal souls in the roaring game so well described in Macbeth's words as "full of sound and fury, signifying nothing."[6]

Today black bonspiels are pretty well limited to Hell.

━━◆◆━━

CAST OF CHARACTERS

O. Cloutie:[7] Travelling man. For untold millennia he has had his own curling rink. He is founder of First Fallen Angel Church, Closed Assembly of Satan. He is a poor loser.

Wullie MacCrimmon: MacCrimmon of the MacCrimmons, Professors of Pibroch,[8] and Pipers to the Chiefs of Scotland. In his late fifties, Wullie is a harness-and-shoe-maker, and a continuing Presbyterian.[9]

---

[4]The Protestant-Catholic conflict in Northern Ireland, particularly violent in the early 1970s, was still raging when Mitchell wrote this tongue-in-cheek introduction in 1982 for Macmillan's *Dramatic W.O. Mitchell*. Both sides used car bombs and targeted civilian areas such as pubs. Reverend Ian Paisley has played a major role in Northern Ireland affairs from the 1950s to the present. He is virulently anti-Catholic and pro-Unionist (i.e., the union of Northern Ireland and Great Britain), and many view his inflammatory rhetoric as a major cause of Northern Ireland's violent and divisive politics over the past half-century.

[5]Sunday, the seventh day of the week (paralleling the seventh day God rested following the six days of creation). The fourth commandment decrees, "Remember the Sabbath to keep it holy," which means no work or other activity should be engaged in on this religious day of rest when one should be paying homage to God.

[6]The Macbeth reference is from *Macbeth* V.v. (see page 80 below).

[7]Old Cloutie, or Auld Cloutie, is a Scots name for the Devil.

[8]Traditional Scots pipe music.

[9]In 1925, four Protestant denominations united to form the United Church of Canada. The largest of these denominations were the Presbyterian Church of Canada and the Methodist Church of Canada. A minority of Presbyterians refused to participate in this union and called themselves continuing Presbyterians (see the exchange between Wullie and Pringle on page 40 below).

He skips his own curling rink.[10] Like O. Cloutie, he prefers to win.

Reverend B.G. Pringle: Early middle age. Skilled curler. Since the union of the Methodist and Presbyterian churches in the twenties, he has been minister of Grace United Church. He does not at all suggest the pulpit in speech or manner.

Annie Brown: Wife of Malleable Charlie Brown. She is Church of Jesus Christ of Latter-Day Saints.[11] She does not curl. A little of Annie Brown goes a long way and there seems to be quite a lot of her. She also is a poor loser.

Pipe-fitting Charlie Brown: Plumber, who curls second for Wullie. He is close to Wullie in age. Over the years, the joints of his Protestant soul have sprung many leaks, but he feels that time and corrosion will heal up anything.

Clock Charlie Brown: A middle-aged jeweller who curls lead for Wullie. He is Catholic.

Malleable Charlie Brown: A middle-aged blacksmith who curls third for Wullie. He has two problems, the first being an untrustworthy lower back, the second being his wife, Annie.

Guy Fawkes:[12] Explosive Englishman, who curls lead for O. Cloutie.

---

[10]A curling team, or rink, consists of four players: the lead, second, third, and skip. They curl their rocks in that order, the skip having the last pair of rocks in each end because he is the most accomplished player both in terms of how accurately he can place his rocks, and in his ability as a tactician (curling is often referred to as "chess on ice").

[11]Mormon Church, founded by Joseph Smith in 1830.

[12]Guy Fawkes was a Roman Catholic revolutionary who was involved in England's Gunpowder Plot of November 5, 1605. An explosives expert, he was put in charge of the gunpowder which was to be used to blow up the Houses of Parliament (hopefully killing James I and destroying his Protestant government). The plot was foiled before it could be carried out. November 5 is Guy Fawkes night in England, an annual celebration of

Judas Iscariot:[13] Lapsed Christian, who curls second for O. Cloutie.

Macbeth:[14] A rather wordy and ambitious countryman of Wullie MacCrimmon, who curls third for O. Cloutie. Like Wullie, he is a continuing Presbyterian. He can appreciate Malleable Charlie Brown's marital problem.

⇒•◆•⇐

ACT I

It is January in the early thirties in the foothills town of Wildrose. Main Street has the false fronts of stores with Wullie MacCrimmon's Shoe and Harness mid-stage between "Steve Hazzard—Licensed Embalmer and Funeral Director" to the left and "Chez Sadie's" beauty parlor.

As the lights come up we see Wullie astride his last[15] as he works at soling a shoe in his shop. Two bearded Hutterites in their sombre clothes and wearing their black caracul[16] pail-shaped winter hats, each of them carrying limp-necked and naked Christmas geese for sale, come down the street.[17] O. Cloutie, on his way to Steve Hazzard's, stops to peer into Wullie's shop. As the Hutterites encounter Mr. Cloutie, a long tail drops out from under his winter coat. They had not really needed the tail to

---

fireworks and bonfires over which effigies of Guy are burned. In one production of *Black Bonspiel*, some stage dirctions had Fawkes periodically producing matches from his pocket, lighting them, and staring at the flame.

[13]Judas Iscariot was the disciple who betrayed Christ. For thirty pieces of silver, he identified Christ to the Roman authorities by giving him a kiss.

[14]The Macbeth of Shakespeare's play. The comparison of Malleable's Annie to Macbeth's Lady Macbeth is the first of Mitchell's incongruously comic allusions to Macbeth. It is the ambitious Lady Macbeth who goads her husband into murdering Duncan, King of Scots, as he sleeps.

[15]Device in the shape of a foot used to hold a shoe in place while it is being worked on.

[16]Persian lamb.

[17]The Manitoba Theatre Centre production had snow falling for the first five minutes of this scene and then a shorter snowfall later in the act when Pipe makes his second entrance (Prompt Script, 1981–82, P 4439, file 16, Archives of Manitoba).

tell them who this stranger is, for ever since the Reformation their Anabaptist sodality[18] has kept up fervent resistance to worldliness; Satan has not done a large-volume business in Amish, Dunkard, Mennonite, or Hutterite souls.[19] Cloutie retrieves his tail and tucks it back up under his topcoat and into his hip pocket. He goes on to enter Steve Hazzard's funeral home.

As organ music takes up "Onward Christian Soldiers," the Reverend Pringle comes down the street from the left and crosses right, where he sees Annie Brown approaching.

Annie: Oh, Mr. Pringle ... *(She takes a couple of quick steps up to him.)* I was hoping I'd run across you ...

Pringle: What is it, Mrs. Brown? *(Pause.)* Now.

Annie: Before Lucy Tregillis—before Lucy—has she talked to you already?

Pringle: About what?

Annie: I mean—Lucy *is* on the Home and School Association ...

Pringle: Yes ...

Annie: But that doesn't mean she is the *whole* Home and School Association ... there *are other* members of the Home and School Association ... just because she *thinks* she is the whole Home and School, that simply does not *make* her the whole Home and School ... even though she acts as though she were the whole Home and School. *(Full stop for a breath initially, but as so*

---

[18]Anabaptists believe that only believing adults should be baptised; a sodality is an association of religious brotherhood (OED).

[19]All Protestant sects with strict religious practices.

many run-on talkers do, Annie has momentarily lost the thread of what she had intended to say.) Ah—oh—yes—it is not simply a matter—a concern—a responsibility—of—the School Board—the teacher ... these are *our* children too! *(Pause.)* Don't you agree?

Pringle: I might ... if I knew what you're driving at.

Annie: Just the corruption of our children!

Theatre Calgary (1979): Stephen Hair as Reverend Pringle;
Sharon Bakker as Annie Brown.

Pringle: *(A little weary.)* You've overheard coarse language on the school grounds again ...

Annie: No—the classrooms!

Pringle: Oh—and Lucy Tregillis is in favour of it.

Annie: No—no—but she certainly is not objective about it when Charlie Tregillis is Principal—conflict ...

Pringle: Between you and Lucy ...

Annie: ... of interest!

Pringle: So—Charlie Tregillis has been using coarse language in the class ...

Annie: No—no ...

Pringle: The children have been ...

Annie: No.

Pringle: Who has?

Annie: *(Flatly serious.)* William Shakespeare for one and somebody named Chaucer—though he's not quite so bad because it's sort of a dialect which makes it harder to understand ...[20]

Pringle: But these are classical literature ...

---

[20]Chaucer's *Canterbury Tales* (1386–1400) was written in Middle English. Obviously, Annie has not read Shakespeare or Chaucer. Through Annie, Mitchell lampoons the do-gooder censors who often do not read the works they attack; rather, they single out particular words and phrases which they deem "filthy" or blasphemous.

Annie: You *have* talked with Lucy Tregillis!

Pringle: No. But I have read William Shakespeare and Geoffrey Chaucer's *Canterbury Tales*. These writers are ...

Annie: Simply filthy.

Pringle: ... earthy—a little bawdy now and again ... yes—filthy—no.

Annie: Yes. The Home and School think they should be removed from the classroom—ah—*most* of the Home and School do ...

Pringle: And—what would the Home and School suggest in their place?

Annie: Nellie McClung—her *Sowing Seeds in Danny*[21] is a beautiful book—and, of course—*Uncle Tom's Cabin* ...[22]

Pringle: *Uncle Tom's Cabin* is obscene.

Annie: *Black Beauty.*[23]

Pringle: Oh, come on, Mrs. Brown—Black Beauty is the most self-centred, self-pitying whiner ... very few horses read her anymore.

---

[21]Nellie McClung's *Sowing Seeds in Danny* (1908) is a sentimental and moral story about a boy growing up.

[22]Harriet Beecher Stowe's *Uncle Tom's Cabin* (1852), a sentimental and moral novel about how Christian love can lead to the abolishment of slavery, had a profound effect on attitudes towards African Americans and slavery in nineteenth-century America. Pringle's dismissal of it as "obscene" reflects a more contemporary critical view of the novel which sees its stereotyping of Blacks as offensive.

[23]Anna Sewell's popular children's story (1877). Black Beauty, a horse, tells the story of his life and sufferings in the London cab trade.

Annie: That's another thing—

Pringle: What is?

Annie: Harness racing. It's taken over the whole town, you
know—the male portion—they gamble—you know—
fast horses—loose women ...

Pringle: I certainly disapprove of gambling—especially on loose
women.

Annie: And curling.

Pringle: *(Seriously.)* Gambling—on curling!

Annie: No. Sabbath curling!

*The door of Steve Hazzard's funeral parlor opens and O. Cloutie, in his
dark fall coat—the tailored kind with a velvet collar—steps out. He wears
a dark homburg hat, and is carrying in one hand a sample case such as
travelling men[24] have for samples of literature and in the other a parcel
wrapped in plain brown paper. He has a dark Vandyke beard[25] and
upward-flaring eyebrows. The door closes carefully behind him by itself.*

Pringle: Oh—I *am* with you on that, Mrs. Brown. We are going
to fight for that by-law—*No* curling on the Sabbath!
And we *are* going to win that!

The Devil has come to them. He tips his homburg to Mrs. Brown.

Devil: 'Day, Mrs. Brown. Mr. Pringle. Nice, crisp day.

---

[24]Salesmen who travel from town to town to sell their goods.
[25]Moustache and beard on the chin named after Anthony van Dyke, a seventeenth-century
Flemish painter.

Theatre Calgary (1979): Michael Ball as the Devil.

He keeps right on going.

Annie: Oh—good afternoon—uh—Mr.—ah—*(She stares after the Devil.)* Well, you're not going to catch my Charlie curling on Sunday—who's that?

Pringle: Stranger to me.

Annie: Addresses you by name. *And* me! I don't know him. Very well dressed—must be a travelling man— probably from Calgary. So, Mr. Pringle—we can count on your support—getting Shakespeare and—ah— Chaucer out of our schools ...

Pringle: No—you can't, Mrs. Brown—but I am behind you in Sunday curling—strongly.

Annie: And Dr. Langley's car.

Pringle: Yes—yes. (*He has turned to leave her, but she has put a hand on his arm.*)

Annie: Buick sedan licence number FUA 4116 with the M after that doctor's ...

Pringle: I'm sure ... (*Again he is trying to get away but she hangs on.*)

Annie: Last two nights it's been parked in front of Mame Harris's house ... the last two nights—

Pringle: Mrs. Brown ...

Annie: —that I know of!

Pringle: Mrs. Brown, being a minister I can't afford a car, but if I could, you would have known its make and licence number and you would have spotted it there too—the last *five* days. Dr. Langley and I both visit the sick—one of Mame Harris's nieces is quite ill—ruptured appendix—it's been touch and go. (*He has freed himself and he strides off.*)

Annie: (*Looking after him.*) Niece—nieces—no woman boards *seven* nieces. Touch and go! I'll bet! (*She starts off in the other direction down the street.*)

Lights up on Wullie MacCrimmon's Shoe and Harness repair shop. Interior: There is a counter separating the workshop and the "public" side of the shop. Wullie is sitting at his shoe last mending a shoe. On the "public" side of the counter at far right is a pot-bellied heater with a mica belly-button, the stovepipe angling in anguish up and across the ceiling, then up and at right angles and out the side wall. At far left of the shop next to Wullie's last is the shoes-to-be-repaired counter in which are tumbled various pairs of ticketed shoes, boots, and slippers. Above the door is a small bell which rings when a customer enters.[26]

The Devil enters, puts the brown parcel he has been carrying on the counter, and opens it.

Wullie looks up from the last. He lays his hammer down. He gets up with the care and preciseness of the rheumatic and walks towards the counter. His face has a full, pursed look. His eyes still on the visitor, he lifts his hand and spits out the cargo of tacks. He places them on the counter.

Wullie: Aye-he?[27]

Devil: My curling boots. I would like a resole job done on them.

The Devil has crossed to the stove and plunged both hands through the opening at the top to warm them. Wullie has not seen this.

Wullie: *(Looking down at the parcel, now suspicious and a little—just a very little—worried.)* When—ah—when would you want them done?

Devil: My next trip through. Two weeks ...

Wullie: You curl. *(Devil nods.)* At the Glencoe? In Calgary?

---

[26]The Manitoba Theatre Centre production worked it so that the bell does not ring when the Devil enters the shop, only when other characters come in (Prompt Script, 1981–82, P 4439, file 16, Archives of Manitoba).

[27]Wullie's pronunciation of the Scots "aye," the equivalent of "yes." Mitchell frequently uses dialect spelling and idioms in his characters' dialogue. Other examples are Grandmother McMurray's Scots dialect in *Who Has Seen the Wind*, Archie Nicotine's Stoney Indian dialect in *The Vanishing Point*, and Wong's Chinese Pidgin English in *The Devil's Instrument*.

Devil: *(Shakes his head.)* No. *(Pause.)* When could you—could I have them in two weeks' time?

Wullie: *(Shrugs toward the shoes-to-be-repaired shelf.)* I'm behind on my repairs. *(He cautiously turns the boots over, using his rasp.)* Nice boots though[28]—yes—uh—afraid you'll have to resort to buckled overshoes for—uh—three weeks?

Devil: *(Calculated pause as he looks at Wullie.)* Three weeks then.

Wullie: Best I can do. You're not from around here then.

Devil: No.

Wullie: I've seen your face before though.

Devil: Quite likely.

Wullie: Foothills Bonspiel?

Devil shakes his head.

Wullie: Little Britches Bullshow, Rodeo, and Craft Fair?

Devil: *(Shakes his head.)* I'm a travelling man.

Wullie: Fooled me—put me in mind of a professional man—more like—oh—university professor—

Devil: *(Laughs.)* Very perceptive. I do a lot of business in Academe.

---

[28]Manitoba Theatre Centre added two speeches here: "Wullie: Custom made?" and "Devil: Italian" (Prompt Script, 1981–82, P 4439, file 16, Archives of Manitoba).

Wullie: I'm not familiar with that town. Aye-he—or—no— politician?

Devil: I spend a lot of time in Ottawa, Edmonton. Three weeks then?

Wullie: Aye-he.

Devil: I had detail work planned for here in two weeks but I'll move it ahead one week, then move right on through and down to Lethbridge. Lethbridge is always rich and rewarding territory.[29]

Wullie: Encyclopedia sets?—I've got it! Bible salesman!

Devil: You really hogged that rock,[30] Wullie! My card. *(He exits.)*[31]

Wullie: *(Picking up a boot.)* Warm—warmer than it would be if he'd just taken it off. But he's carried them outside and it's twenty below. *(Picks up the business card and reads aloud.)* Mr. O. Cloutie, Wholesale Souls, Retail Sins. Business and Home Address: Sulphur Blvd., Hell. *(Pause.)* Ah, well. A boot's a boot for all that.[32]

---

[29]In the Manitoba Theatre Centre production, Lethbridge becomes Winnipeg (Prompt Script, 1981–82, P 4439, file 16, Archives of Manitoba); in the 1984 Kawartha Festival production, the Lindsay audience delighted in the Devil's referring to Peterborough as "rich and rewarding territory" (Sprung, 314).

[30]Curling term for a rock that does not make it to the hog line, which is twenty-one feet in front of the house's centre, the one-foot button. The curler slides his rock (a forty-four pound polished granite stone with a handle on top) from the far end of the rink attempting to place his rock in the house, the target area. Rocks that do not cross the hog line are taken out of play.

[31]Manitoba Theatre Centre adds Devil saying, "BIBLE SALESMAN!" as he exits (Prompt Script, 1981–82, P 4439, file 16, Archives of Manitoba).

[32]A play on Robert Burns' poem, "A Man's a Man for a' That" ("a' That" referring to social status).

>(*Carelessly, and with contempt for all people in high places, even though their title be the Prince of Darkness, he negligently tosses the boots onto the shelf. He walks to the last, sits, takes up his hammer, and begins the crooked rhythm of shoe repairing.*)

For a few moments the Devil's curling boots simply lie on the pile of laborers' felt boots, high-heeled riding-boots, somehow pathetic little child's boots, boots with great bunion bulges. Then, as Wullie's hammer continues its tapping impatience, the Devil's curling boots almost seem to glow. Imperceptibly at first, they steam, then from them lifts a definite drifting wraith of smoke.

Wullie: Sulphur Blvd. (*Pause.*) Hell!

The Reverend B.G. Pringle is just closing the door. He is a progressive United Church minister. He is thirty-five—still plays a little hockey with the young people. He is a quite nice, straight young man—not a precious-spinster caricature.

Pringle: Always the warm greeting, Mr. MacCrimmon.

Wullie: Reverend—no offence intended. You may help yourself to a cup of coffee.

Pringle: No thanks. Are you busy?

Wullie: Some. You're not the first.

Pringle: First?

Wullie: Visitor. (*Looks up at Pringle.*) Had your opposition in just now.

Pringle: Oh—oh—was Father O'Halloran here to visit?

Wullie: No—no. *(Pause.)* What had you in mind, Mr. Pringle?

Pringle: *(He is obviously embarrassed.)* Oh—a moment—just a moment of your time. Ah—called on Mr. Clayton and uh—Mr. Thompson—Mr. Bolley.

Wullie stares hard at Mr. Pringle.

Wullie: All members of your congregation.

Pringle: Yes. *(Not important really.)* Yes—they are. *(Awkward pause.)* Mr. MacCrimmon—*(Clears throat.)* I know you aren't a member of Grace—of our church.

Wullie: That's right.

Pringle: Still—I am calling on you just as I did on the others—uh—in regard to the new church.

Wullie: Aye-he. *(He puts a boot over the last, puts tacks back into his mouth, picks up the hammer.)*

Pringle: We hope to break—ground on it early this spring.

Wullie: Do you. *(He knows what's coming and he begins to hammer on the shoe. Continues through.)*

Pringle: When we have managed the necessary funds. *(Pause.)* When we have managed the necessary funds. *(Quite pointed.)*

Wullie: Mmmmmmmm-mh.

Pringle: *(Brightly.)* So far we have done very well—almost better than we expected. And—ah—I see one of my fondest dreams very near to coming true. The thing I've directed all my energies towards since coming to Wildrose.

Wullie: That an' prohibition ...

Pringle: Yes. In the matter of temperance I have taken a firm stand.

Wullie   The prohibition of Sabbath curling.

Pringle: *(Crossing to stove.)* Oh—yes—that—yes. *(Awkward pause.)* I've always felt that there should be one day set aside for the spirit.

Wullie   You could say curling was as much for the spirit as for the flesh ...

Pringle: Well—for—for—contemplation. One day out of seven for—uh—I—well, I suppose we do not see eye to eye on that, Mr. MacCrimmon. *(Crosses back to counter.)*

Wullie   No—we do not.

Pringle: But you must admit that we will probably get the approval of a majority of the townspeople. More against Sunday curling than ...

Wullie   Because more do not curl than do ... or have wives that do not. Not one curler will vote for your by-law prohibiting Sabbath curling.

Pringle: For their own good, Mr. MacCrimmon. For their own good.

Wullie   You can't.

Pringle: Can't what?

Wullie: You can't determine for other people what's for their own good. It's a judgment they must acquire for themselves.

Pringle: Oh now ... it often helps to have a little outside help now and again. No harm in stiffening the moral ...

Wullie: If it needs outside stiffening, it is then a false morality. You could patch up the outside from now till the resurrection[33] and you would still have a poor thing, Mr. Pringle. *(Picking up a shoe and sticking his fingers through a hole in the sole.)* Have you tried to work from the inside out, Mr. Pringle?

Pringle: We do that—we do that too.

Wullie: Do you now.

Pringle: *(Opening his ledger and unscrewing his fountain pen.)* Now—I know you are not a member of our congregation but—I—have—I would like to put your name down.

Wullie: *(He is now on the other side of the counter facing Pringle.)* Mr. Pringle.

Pringle: *(Looking up but with the pen nib poised.)* Yes?

Wullie: You know I was born Presbyterian.

Pringle: Yes ...

---

[33]Refers to the Christian belief in the resurrection of the dead at the end of the world.

Wullie: As you were.

Pringle: Well, I ...

Wullie: But with this difference—I still am—Presbyterian. Continuing Presbyterian.

Pringle: But we welcome—you're welcome to come and worship with us in Grace United.

Wullie: No thanks. When it was Grace Presbyterian—that was another thing—but now that it has turned—*(Pause for emphasis while Wullie's face shows his distaste as though the word were sour in his mouth.)* Methodist!

Pringle: Not Methodist. It isn't Methodist, Mr. MacCrimmon. United!

Wullie: I was not born nor was I brought up Methodist. *(Brings down cobbling hammer smartly on the counter, barely missing Pringle's hand.)* I do not intend to live Methodist. *(Crosses back to last.)*

Pringle: Now just a minute—you've started out with the wrong assumption ...

Wullie: I have been given the choice of your Methodist Church and ...

Pringle: *(Objecting noises.)* Oh, please ...

Wullie: *(Magnanimously.)* All right—all right, your United Church—Baptist—Seventh Day Advent—Jesus Christ of the Latter-Day Saints—Father O'Halloran's Saint Theresa and the Meetings of the Burning Church of

Nazareth over the Odd Fellows Hall. *(Pause.)* I have visited them all since, since ...

Pringle: Since the union.

Wullie: Since the loss of my own church. *(Pause.)* I long ago decided to remain what I am—continuing Presbyterian with the creed of my fathers, and what was a good foundation for my father is a good foundation for me.

Pringle: But your father lived in a different world. Your father believed many things that you don't believe in.

Wullie: No. My faith and my convictions are the same as my father's—the same as the day I sat beside him in church—hearing the minister's voice soaring and dipping grand as he painted for his congregation the hell that awaited all sinners. *(He has crossed to the stove.)*

Pringle: We believe in a religion of love today, Mr. MacCrimmon.

Wullie: *(Pokes fire with poker.)* Aye—of love and no Hell.

Pringle: Well ...

Wullie: ... and no Devil.

Pringle: Symbolically speaking.

Wullie: I mean actually speaking. Hell and the Devil. There's the foundation for a religion—the skeletal require- ments you might say. Mr. Pringle, when you begin to preach sermons with some bones in them, when you can show me something besides the wishy-washy symbolical hells and symbolical devils—then Wullie MacCrimmon will be right alongside the other members of your congregation—taking communion with—in your new Methodist church!

Pringle: *(Wullie turns his back on him and picks up a chunk of wood.)* But it's not Methodist—it's United—oh all right, Mr. MacCrimmon. *(He turns back to the counter, picks up his ledger, and begins to fold it closed.)* I'll—I won't bother to put your name down.

Wullie: Hold on now. Don't be too hasty. Half a loaf is better than none. I don't mind ...

Pringle: Half a loaf!

Wullie: How much had you in mind putting me down for?

Pringle: Twenty dollars.

Wullie: I see. *(Pause.)* A church is a church. *(Pause.)* Methodist or not.

Pringle: But it's ...

Wullie: Twenty dollars. An indirect blow.

Pringle: Indirect blow!

Wullie: Mr. Pringle. Please sit down. *(Wullie sits on other chair next to Pringle.)* Will you tell me one thing.

Pringle: Yes?

Wullie: Do you or do you not believe in a devil?

Pringle: *(Finds this question a rough one.)* Well—*(Long pause.)* I do believe there is a force for evil abroad in the world.

Wullie: That does not answer my question. Do you believe in a personal Devil?

Pringle: Well—*(Longer pause.)* I—*(Clears his throat.)* No.

Wullie: Do you believe in Hell?[34]

Pringle: *(Long pause—clears his throat.)*

Wullie: Do—you—believe—in Hell?

Pringle: I believe we make a hell for ourselves through our ...

Wullie: Ah! *(Rising and opening the stove door.)* Do you believe in a three-dimensional, crackling, actually burning Hell to which we may or we may not go—when our time comes? Where we may roast in blazing fire from everlasting to everlasting? Do you? Shrieking and writhing in torment and exquisite pain beyond all human comprehension while the Lord—in His infinite compassion and mercy—looks down from the dew-washed heights of Heaven above.[35]

Pringle: *(Finds this utterly repugnant to his notion of a Heavenly Father and true Christianity.)* No! Mr. MacCrimmon, no. I do not!

---

[34]The 1986 Neptune Theatre production added a stage direction here, "*Opens stove*" (Prompt Script, 1986, MS-3-1, Box 283, File 10, Neptune Theatre, Dalhousie University Archives). Note how the stove in this scene becomes a "symbolical" presence.

[35]Manitoba Theatre Centre adds, "Do you?" (Prompt Script, 1981–82, P 4439, file 16, Archives of Manitoba).

Wullie: *(Bangs home the wood chunk into the flames.)* Aye-he. *(He clangs the door shut and turns back to Pringle.)* And what would you say, Mr. Pringle, *(Wullie crosses behind the counter and leans over it to Pringle.)* if one day you sat in your study with the King James version of the Bible in one hand—your thumb and finger in the Concordance[36]—and there came a ring at the doorbell? What would you say if you went to it and found there a dark gentleman—black brows that turned upwards at their outer corners? If you saw that he had hoofs ...

Pringle: Oh—now—now ...

Wullie: And he announced himself as the Devil come to have a short talk with you between his routine calls in the town of Wildrose, Alberta?

Pringle: I'd say I was having hallucinations.

Wullie: Then you would be wrong. Now there is where Father O'Halloran and I come a little closer to understanding each other. I remember his explaining to me about a year ago the meaning of a Black Mass.

Pringle: Black Mass!

Wullie: Then you've heard of it.

Pringle: I believe that in more backward countries—ignorant and superstitious people ...

Wullie: A ceremony devoted to the worship of the Devil— everything backwards—robes worn backwards— crucifix upside down—prayers backwards. Black Mass.

---

[36]Alphabetical index of words in the Bible listing each word's appearances and contexts.

Pringle: Superstition!

Wullie: 'Tis an old superstition then.

Pringle: It's still ...

Wullie: As old as time. *(He goes towards the last.)* As old as the Flesh. As old as Adam. *(He sits down at the last.)* And you think you'd be having hallucinations if you saw Old Cloutie ...

Pringle: Yes—I certainly ...

Wullie: Then you would be wrong. I know. He called on me today.

Pringle: What!

Wullie: In the shop here. Brought me in a pair of his curling boots for me to mend.

Pringle: That's ridic—

Wullie: Oh no it isn't. *(Gestures with his head towards the shoes-to-be-repaired shelf.)* They lie over there on top of the shoes to be repaired ...

Pringle: *(Laughing.)* A devil bringing in curling boots.

Wullie: Aye-he, it's unusual—most curlers just use overshoes. You don't find many custom-made curling boots.

Pringle: Nor devils who curl. What would bring him here?

Wullie: He tells me he's a regular visitor here in Wildrose. He'll be back in three weeks' time.

Pringle: *(Rising and crossing to counter for ledger.)* I knew you were a stubborn man, Mr. MacCrimmon—I knew you were—uh—old-fashioned—in your beliefs—but I never ever did you the—I never for a moment accused you of being superstitious.

Wullie: And I'm not. *(He gets up from the last, walks silently to the cash box he has under the counter.)* Now—twenty dollars.

Pringle: Eh?

Wullie: Towards your new Methodist church. If he's a regular visitor to Wildrose, we could use another church—new church. You may put me down for twenty dollars. *(He looks down as he thumbs over the bills in his hand.)* I'm going to need all the support I can get ... *(Sticks out the twenty dollars at Pringle, who takes them numbly.)* however unpromising it may look. Here.

Pringle will never understand the dark ways of the heart of a dour Scot. Bewildered, he slowly, sadly shakes his head and goes out.

Mrs. Annie Brown enters.

Annie: You just had a visitor.

Wullie: Aye—he—Reverend Pringle.

Annie: No—no—distinguished gentleman.

Wullie: Oh—him.

Annie: Not from Wildrose.

Wullie: No.

Manitoba Theatre Centre (1982):
Wayne Robson as Wullie; Nancy Drake as Annie Brown.

Annie: He knew me by name.

Wullie: I'm not surprised.

Annie: And Mr. Pringle.

Wullie: They're both in the same business—you might say.

Annie: Oh—oh—he's a man of the cloth.

Wullie: Not quite.

Annie: Well—he is or he isn't.

Wullie: He is concerned with souls. And I don't mean *leather* ones. Was there a nice *serious* reason you dropped in, Mrs. Brown?

Annie: Yes. The curling by-laws. You *are* a moral man. *(Wullie just stares at her.)* Christian.

Wullie: *(Pause.)* Continuing Presbyterian—

Annie: And—He labored six days and on the Seventh Day He rested and the eighth commandment says to keep His Sabbath holy—doesn't it?

Wullie: Sixth—[37]

Annie: Oh—it does seem strange to me that you do not seem to support the by-law to prohibit Sunday curling.

Wullie: I do not consider curling—on any day—a profanin' or corruptin' pursuit—and really, Mrs. Brown—it is none of your business at all.

Annie: Well it is—as long as my husband curls third on your rink.

Wullie: *His* yes—yours—no. For you do not curl third on my rink.

She hasn't a reply to that yet. The door has opened and Pipe-fitting Brown has come in.

Pipe: Mrs. Brown—your waste-an'-overflow[38] got plugged up again?

Annie looks at him, then back to Wullie. Decides both are impossible. She leaves.

---

[37]Keeping the Sabbath is actually the fourth commandment. See Annie's and Pringle's exchange on page 87 below.

[38]Drain and overflow set-up for a toilet or bath tub.

Neptune Theatre (1986): Catherine McKinnon as Annie Brown;
Don Harron as Wullie; Glen White as Reverend Pringle.

*Pipe-fitting, with automatic precision from old habit, goes to coffee pot
on Quebec-heater top, reaches under counter for a mug, and, pouring,*

Pipe: ... five times she's called me up there. Five times I
              unplugged her—an' five times I told her all she's got to
              do is stop little Byron from droppin' his Plasticine
              down an' she won't get plugged an' I won't have to haul
              my tools up there an' unplug her. That's the trouble
              with plumbing, Wullie—all the time dealing with the
              public—female public.

Wullie: Aye-he. *(Wullie has now returned to his shoe repair.)*

Pipe: *(Has prepared two mugs of coffee. Sits on chair.)* That's
              where Malleable Brown has it all over me—black-
              smithin' you don't get many women walkin' in an'

askin' you to do a job for 'em with them breathin'
down your neck. Don't find him tanglin' with the
female public way I do. Some. Not one hundred
percent the time. Gets on a person's nerves ...

Wullie:: Aye-he.

Pipe: Look at me—how many years I bin curlin' second for
you?

Wullie: Twenty-two.

Pipe: An' I should of bin skippin' a rink for twenty-two
years—just one reason why I didn't—nerves—
plumber's nerves. Loose as the fringe on a Indian jacket.
I say you can't have iron nerves an' be a plumber—an'
you can't skip unless you got iron nerves.

Wullie: You're a good second, Pipe-fitting.

Pipe: We're all good, Wullie. You're skippin' the best rink in
Wildrose, Wullie.

Wullie: (*Why argue—it's the truth.*) Aye-he.

Pipe: Malleable Charlie Brown's a nice third—except for
when that back goes out on him. Clock Charlie Brown's
a dandy lead, except for when he gets to thinking he's
skip—an' we all bin curlin' together over twenty years.
An' this year we're better'n we ever bin before. Why
look at last night—after the fourth end[39] Doc Hanley

---

[39]A game of curling involves ten ends (unless the score is tied in which case it goes to extra
ends). An end consists of each player curling two rocks. After each end, scoring rocks are
tallied, the result entered on the scoreboard, and a new end begins with players now curling
their rocks towards the house at the opposite end of the rink.

Neptune Theatre (1986): Don Harron as Wullie; Bill Carr as Pipe.

didn't have no more chance than a gopher through a twenty-six-inch thrashing machine. Way we're curlin' this year we could take the Macdonald Brier. How'd you like to curl the Macdonald Brier,[40] Wullie?

Wullie slowly sits himself down at his last. His gaze becomes distant. In the background we hear a slow fade up of "The Maple Leaf Forever."[41]

Wullie: The Macdonald Brier. *(This is almost whispered with reverence.)* Aye-he, the Macdonald Brier ...

Pipe: I seen 'em once. 'Thirty-two—time they played off at the Glenmore Club ...

---

[40]The Canadian National Curling Championship was sponsored by Macdonald Tobacco from 1927 to 1977.

[41]For several years the unofficial Canadian anthem, written by Alexander Muir in 1867 (year of Confederation).

Wullie is smiling gently. Slowly, slowly he closes his eyes. Music is still in background.

Pipe: I never thought I'd ever see 'em, but I did—in 'thirty-two at the Glenmore Club, Edmonton.

The lights fade out except for a spot on Wullie. Music is now fully in as we hear:

Announcer: Ay-announcing thee winner ... Grand Champeens of the Macdonald Brier Playoffs ... champeens by one rock of thee Dominyun of ... Canada ... and ... therefore of thee world ... Skip ... Wullie ... MacCrimmon and his rink made up of ... Lead: Clock Charlie Brown ... Second: Pipe-fitting Charlie Brown ... Third: Malleable Charlie Brown ... all of Wildrose, Alberta, Canada ... *(Cheers.)* And now ... by His Governor-Generalship, the Governor General of Canada ... thee presentation of the Macdonald Brier Cup and special souvenirs ... for each man a gold spittoon from the Senate ... engraved with their names. *(Pause.)* The Governor General!

"The Maple Leaf Forever" has faded out and we now hear bagpipes in the background playing the pibroch.

Gov. Gen.: It gives me very great pleasure in the name of His Majesty—to present these gold Senate spittoons to each of you Charlie Browns of the Wildrose champion rink—and *(Hesitates.)* to your Skip, Wullie MacCrimmon—*(Aside.)* eighteen-carat—not plated—and to have you as my guests in the vice-regal section of the Senate cafeteria for a three-course banquet in your honour, roast mallard, wild rice—moose steaks and mushrooms. *(Pause.)* And smoked Winnipeg gold-eye.

"The Maple Leaf Forever" returns full force as the lights go to black.

When the lights come up again, it is two weeks later and we see Wullie alone in his shop. It is blowing snow outside. Pipe-fitting enters, stamping his feet.

Pipe: Jesus, colder'n the tip of a polar bear's—

Wullie: Aye-he. *(He sets out coffee mugs on counter for Pipe-fitting to pour.)*

Pipe: *(Warming himself by the stove.)* Highwood River's froze tighter'n a bull's ass in fly-time.

Wullie: Aye-he.

Pipe: *(Looking out window.)* Looks like Old King Winter has covered all 'a Wildrose and District with a pure an' snowy blanket.

Wullie: You always do keep your eyes peeled, Pipe-fitting.

Pipe: *(Pours two mugs of coffee, then sits in chair by the stove.)* Gonna be some great curlin' now, Wullie.

Wullie: Aye-he.

Pipe: Wullie.

Wullie: Aye-he.

Pipe: I dreamed over that Dominion Finals we seen in 1932.

Wullie: 'Thirty-three.

Pipe: Edmonton.

Wullie: Calgary.

Pipe: Glenmore Club.

Wullie: Glencoe.

Pipe: Yeah—yeah. That last winning rock in the tenth end.

Wullie: *(Now sitting at his last.)* Eleventh.

Pipe: Straight handle.[42]

Wullie: Aye-he.

Pipe: Knock-out.[43]

Wullie: Aye-he.

Pipe: Right down the sheet—true and sweet and straighter than a Baptist fart through a brass curtain rod!

Wullie: It was—it was! Pipe-fitting—

Pipe: Yeah?

Wullie: I would give anything ... *(Low and reverent.)* utterly anything for to skip the winning rink in the Macdonald Brier Finals—I would give ...

The Devil has entered. In a loud, clear, decisive voice:[44]

---

[42] A rock that has no clockwise or counterclockwise rotation and therefore does not curl.

[43] A rock that is delivered with speed so that it knocks an opposing team's rock out of play.

[44] Most productions have the Devil suddenly appear in a flash of fire here.

Devil: That's a bargain, Wullie MacCrimmon.

Pipe-fitting's mouth has dropped open.

Pipe: Huh!

Devil: *(As before.)* That is a bargain—Wullie MacCrimmon!

All of them in arrested position. The Devil leaning across the counter.

Wullie: *(After a pause.)* Pipe-fitting, would you mind giving a bit of a twist to yon damper on the stovepipe?

The Devil with Pipe-fitting's and Wullie's eyes following him, steps to stove, reaches up and twists the protesting damper. He also pours himself a cup of coffee.

Wullie: —wee bit close in here. *(Pause.)* Pipe-fitting—meet Old Cloutie.

Pipe: *(Half risen from his chair.)* Old Cloutie?

Wullie: Beezalie Bub—Satan—Old Scratch—Old Nick—the Devil—Old Cloutie. *(On this final one, Pipe-fitting falls back down in his chair.)*

Pipe: Oh—*(Pause.)* him. *(He relaxes somewhat in his chair.)* Pleasure. *(Tight-lipped but giving the Devil a chance to be a good guy.)*

Devil: *(Slight bow.)* All mine.

Pipe: How's things?

Devil: Things are all right.

Pipe: Guess the Depression[45] ain't reached—ah—down there yet.

Devil shakes his head.

Pipe: No missions—salt cod—relief trains.[46]

Devil: No idle hands.

Pipe: Hmh. First *good* thing I ever heard about—it.

Devil: In some ways—you might find it pleasant.

Pipe: Ohhh—I don't think—maybe—to *visit* but not to ...

Devil: We curl.

Pipe: *(That makes him forget his discomfort.)* You do!

Wullie looks up from his last.

Wullie: Just for curiosity's sake—how—in Hell do you keep your ice?[47]

Devil: Artificial!

Pipe: Artificial!

---

[45]The play is set in the 1930s Great Depression, sparked off by the stock market crash in 1929. In the prairie provinces, the depression was exacerbated by drought and dust bowl storms. A global economic disaster, the Depression hit Canada and the United States hardest.

[46]Missions or churches gave food and shelter to the unemployed (who in return had to listen to sermons); salt-cod was shipped to the prairies from Newfoundland; relief trains from the east brought free food and supplies to the prairies.

[47]Neptune Theatre stage direction: "*Devil sits on stove*" (Prompt Script, 1986, MS-3-1, Box 283, File 10, Neptune Theatre, Dalhousie University Archives).

Devil: Basaltic[48] sheets. Volcanic deposit. Highly polished—
which gives us a fast knock-out game.

Pipe: Yeaaah—mainly shirt-sleeve bonspiels.

Devil: That's right.

Pipe: Sounds all right—*(Qualifying that.)* the—curling part
of it.

Devil: We do have some drawbacks. Hell is a one-resource
economy.

Wullie: Sin.

Devil: Well—yes—there's always that. But sin is an infinitely
renewable commodity. I was thinking of *non-*
renewable *natural* resources. When you people finally
run out of energy—oil—gas—and the way you're
wasting it—you're going to look elsewhere for your
fuel and heat. *(He pauses, then lifts a finger and slowly
tips it to point straight down.)* Deep thermal energy—
mine. It is all mine! Hell was given to me when I was
cast out of Heaven! Hell, including all surface *and*
mineral rights, is my province! When your time of
energy need comes—I will grant no leases—release no
territorial rights or powers of decisions over my *one*,
non-renewable resource, because when that brimstone
runs out, I do not see how—in Hell—we can diversify
our economy. And when the brimstone runs out—
since we could not diversify—I don't know what—in
Hell—we can do! *(He gets a grip on his emotions.)* We

---

[48]Basalt is rock formed from volcanic lava.

have an expression down below: "Let those upper bastards freeze in the dark."[49]

Pipe: Don't sound too neighbourly to me.

Devil: In my situation—you might just change your mind.

Pipe: *(Suddenly remembering his manners, shoves chair at the Devil.)* Take my seat. *(Awkward pause.)* You—uh—two got business—I'll—I'll—be goin'. *(Picking up his tools.)* It was Wullie you wanted to have a talk with ...

Devil: That's right.

Pipe: Never did get around to finishin' up Mrs. Harrison's waste-an'-overflow. Guess I better get hold of my wrenches an' skin over there. *(He slams the door as he exits.)*

Wullie: You're early.

Devil: Came through on an unscheduled trip involving an ungraded school teacher[50] and some beer.

Wullie: That would be Miss Sparrow—been going into the Ladies and Escorts room[51] of the Royal Hotel with the new Royal Bank cashier.

---

[49]Mitchell, whose political leanings were liberal and federalist, frequently took satirical aim at the parochial and self-serving politics of Social Credit and Conservative Albertans. In the Devil's speech here, he is sending up Ralph Klein who, when mayor of Calgary in 1980, coined the slogan, "Let the eastern bastards freeze in the dark" (which sparked off a provincial campaign against the Trudeau government's National Energy Program).

[50]Teachers who were unqualified and hired on a temporary basis.

[51]Unless accompanied by a male, women were not allowed in beer parlours and only then in the "Ladies and Escorts" room, which was separate from the main beer parlour.

Manitoba Theatre Centre (1982):
Wayne Robson as Wullie; Robert Benson as the Devil.

Devil: That's right.

Wullie: Small matter—isn't it?

Devil: In itself—yes. (*He has set his case on one chair and sits in the other, looking through his file cards.*) Mrs. Sadie Burbidge saw her go in—she mentioned it to Mrs. Annie Brown, who in turn got on the phone the greater part of yesterday. Mrs. Brown looks interesting to me.

Wullie: Uh-huh ...

Devil: Most interesting.

Wullie: Just argy-bargy,[52] isn't it?

---

[52]Scots for quarreling, haggling.

Devil: In itself—yes. But this woman—with her it's the accretion that counts.

Wullie: I see.

Devil: *(He is now looking through a note pad.)* For the most part nothing very flashy in the way of sin goes on in Wildrose. My regular calls are the Blue Bird Café—penny ante in the little back room. Mame Harris's little brown cottage by the CPR depot is a routine call of mine—then there's the pool hall.

Wullie: Aye-he.

Devil: The small novelty line. Petty intolerance—lust for teapot power—self-indulgence—sins of omission—snobbery—within-the-family tyranny—*(Pause.)* that sort of thing—*(Deprecatory.)* quick turn-over. *(Sighs.)*

Wullie: I take it—all's not well—in Hell.

Devil: All *is* well in Hell. It's up here—sometimes I ask myself—just what am I doing—up on the territory again—century after century selling sin. After millennia of calls and eons of detail work all my lines are well established—but it's the same old inventory. You think it's a challenge to sell gluttony today—avarice. Sloth? Lust—lust just sells itself. And the quality of sinner. They simply do not make sinners the way they used to. No style. *(Pause.)* But that's the short-term view. Long term? Prospects are good. I'm quite optimistic about one—on the continent—ludicrous little one-balled paperhanger and painter—of all people—he looks most

Neptune Theatre (1986):
Don Harron as Wullie; Maxim Mazumdar as the Devil.

promising.[53] Also—I see a great future for three
items not even included in the top deadly seven:[54]
bigotry—fanaticism—hypocrisy. Never sell them
short—especially hypocrisy.

Wullie: Mr. Cloutie, I'm sure you did not drop by simply for—
to confide in me more than I really cared to hear. You
did mention a bargain.

---

[53]This refers to Hitler who, as a youth, was trained in the painting and wallpaper trade.
"One-balled" refers to the song World War II troops used to sing, to the tune of the Colonel
Bogey March, about Hitler and his top commanders: "Hitler has only got one ball / Göring
has two but very small, / Himmler is somewhat sim'lar, / And Goebbels has no balls at all."
[54]The seven deadly sins: lust, gluttony, greed, sloth, wrath, envy, and pride.

Devil: I did. *(He brings a contract out of his attaché case and lays it on the counter before Wullie.)* I just happened to bring a contract with me—look it over. *(Wullie begins to read it.)* My standard soul-for-fair-recompense contract. Stood the test of time because it protects the interests of both parties. No ambiguity because it doesn't oversimplify—nor does it bog down in hair-splitting detail obscuring the intent of the agreement.

Wullie: My soul for the Macdonald Brier Championship.

Devil: That's the deal.

Wullie: *(Long pause as he thinks it over.)* Seems like a fair enough exchange.

Devil: It's a good bargain, Wullie. For both sides.

Wullie: What makes you so fussy about a MacCrimmon soul?

Devil: I might as well be frank with you ... I need a good third for my rink.

Wullie: *You do?*

Devil: You've always dreamed of curling in the Macdonald Brier. Since long before the ice age I've wanted to win a championship bonspiel—The Celestial Brier Playoffs. I can win it—with you curling third for me.

Wullie: *(Pause as this sinks in.)* Like I said, you arrived early— you caught me unawares.

Devil: I did.

Wullie: Which means—I'm not bound by any verbal contract. So—I would be within my rights if I refused to sign this—written contract.

Devil: You—would—be. *(Grudgingly.)*

Wullie: All right then. *(He shoves the contract towards the Devil.)* I'll not sign that.

Devil: The deal's off?

Wullie: I did not say that. I said—I'll not sign that.

Devil: Oh.

Wullie: As it stands.

Devil: Oh. *(Relief.)* With changes?

Wullie: You might call it a counter-proposition. I have a fair rink of my own. I can't say I'd care to curl third on a rink that couldn't beat the one I now skip. I'd be willing to curl for you in Hell only on the condition that your rink is a better one than mine—the one made up of Clock Brown—Malleable Charlie Brown— Pipe-fitting Charlie Brown.

Devil: *(Still weary.)* And your proposition?

Wullie: You curl us a match. *(Pause.)* If we lose, then I curl third for you at no price—when my time comes ...

Devil: At no price! *(He begins to change the contract.)*

Wullie: Aye-he. You need not deliver me the Macdonald Brier Championships. But—if we win—then you must deliver according to the terms of your first offer. I will skip a winning rink in the Macdonald Brier Playoffs—but again—at no price.

Devil: Now—I want to make this thing perfectly clear. If you win, *you retain your soul?*

Wullie: I retain my soul.

Devil: You sincerely mean that?

Wullie: I do.

Devil: *(Finishing off the amendment.)* " ... party of the second part shall retain his soul."

Wullie: Intact!

Devil: *(Making the correction.)* "Intact."

Wullie: Retains his MacCrimmon soul—intact.

Devil: *(Making the added correction.)* " ... his MacCrimmon soul—intact."

Wullie: The match to be curled on our own ice, of course.

Devil: That's all right.

Wullie: It isn't binding to any other member of my rink, you understand.

Devil: That's right.

Wullie: It'll have to be curled on a Sabbath evening.

Devil: I curl only on the Sabbath.[55] *(Shoves the contract over to Wullie.)* Initial the changes and sign. I already have.

Wullie takes the pen[56] and, after a slight hesitation and glance upwards, initials and signs the contract.

Devil: *(Separating the pages.)* Original for you. *(Hands to Wullie.)* Carbon for me. *(He tucks it into the attaché case.)* Oh—my boots.

Wullie: I'll get to them immediately. Done by the Sabbath next.

Devil: Next Sabbath it is. You've exchanged a good bargain for a bad one, Wullie MacCrimmon.

Wullie: We'll see—in four days.

At that the Devil disappears in a huge cloud of smoke and flame accompanied by a lambasting blast of thunder.

As the lights come up we see Wullie sitting at his last, and Pipe-fitting enters. At the door he peers anxiously, sees Wullie.

Pipe: You—you all right, Wullie?

Wullie: Aye-he. *(Pause.)* He just left.

---

[55]The Devil, in revenge for being cast out of Heaven, is particularly keen to "score" by tempting souls away from God on this holiest of days on which man celebrates his connection with God.

[56]Neptune Theatre has the Devil and Wullie sign the contract with the end of the Devil's tail which flashes when Wullie signs (Prompt Script, 1986, MS-3-1, Box 283, File 10, Neptune Theatre Dalhousie, University Archives).

Pipe: *(To the counter.)* That's nice.

Wullie: *(Returning to his shoe repair.)* And how's Mrs. Harrison's waste-and-overflow?

Pipe: Fine—just fine. Never shed a tear. *(Pause.)* Now. *(Clears his throat.)* You—uh—finished with your—with what you was doing?

Wullie: Aye-he.

Pipe: *(Pause.)* Dripping.

Wullie: Oh.

Pipe: Wasn't nothin' had to be done. C'rosion. C'rosion would of taken care of her. *(Looks speculatively over to Wullie.)* Funny thing about plumbin'. Time. C'rosion. Take care of just about fifty percent of your leaks. *(Still marking time and waiting for Wullie to say something about the visitor.)* Why, I seen new jobs sprayin' at every joint—I seen 'em tighten up by themselves—without a wrench—*(Long pause.)* C'rosion.

Wullie is still working.

Pipe: You—ah—what—maybe it's none of my business—but just what business did he have with you? *(Wullie tosses the curling boots on the counter.)* Curling boots!

Wullie: This was not his first call—couple of weeks ago. He left his curling boots—custom-made—wanted the soles mended. Dropped back a wee bit early to—ah—said he had a little business with Miss Sparrow.

Pipe: *(Relieved.)* Oh. That all?

Wullie: Well—no—it isn't, Pipe-fitting. It isn't all. It isn't all. *(Clears his throat.)* He's quite fussy about curling.

Pipe: I heard. Did you an' him—ah—talk curlin'?

Wullie: We did.

Pipe: Them boots. Was that all he come in for—an' to talk curlin'?

Wullie: No. No. *(Wullie crosses to the counter to face Pipe-fitting.)* He says he has not a particularly good third. He—he's looking for a good third for his rink. He likes my game.

Pipe: Uh-huh.

Wullie: So—it wasn't just the curling boots. He had a proposition to make me. I sort of liked it.

Pipe: Get into an aitch of a mess takin' the Devil up on a proposition, Wullie.

Wullie: Aye-he. This one involved a curling-match. *(Pause to send out a feeler with Pipe-fitting.)* His rink against ours. *(Assessing Pipe-fitting's response.)* Pipe-fitting—if you're willing, I'll be wanting you for a match this Sabbath evening.

Pipe: Agin—agin?

Wullie: Against Old Cloutie and his rink from Hell.

Pipe: *(We see only a momentary hesitation on Pipe-fitting's face.)* Why—sure. Look—I'll tell Malleable for you—let Clock ride, him being Catholic. I figure he'd keep goin' once he got started. That's the way to do her ... *(He* *starts to the door but turns back.)* Kind of curious—see who he's got on his rink. You know—local folks. Take old man Dowling went West in 'thirty-two just after he diddled Mrs. Fowler out of the correction line, sixty acres. *(And he crosses to the door but sees Malleable Charlie Brown on his way to the shop. He and Wullie take "casual" positions on either side of the counter. Malleable enters and crosses to the stove to warm his hands.)*

Pipe: Oh—Malleable—I was just headed your way ...

Malleable: 'Day, Pipe-fitting—Wullie. *(Looking over at the two of them.)* What you Indians been plottin' agin the whites today?

Pipe: Ah—*(Clears throat.)* All—Wullie—me an' Wullie just been talking over a match—Sunday night.

Malleable: Sunday night. Ain't any Sunday curlin'. Reverend Pringle fixed that.

Pipe: This is just a little pick-up match, Malleable. Wullie here made the arrangements. Keepin' it quiet. *(Pause.)* You interested?

Malleable: *(Sliding a plug out of his pocket.)* Sure. *(He opens his jack-knife.)* Who's she agin?

Wullie: Old Cloutie.

Malleable: *(He has the plug between thumb and knife blade—cuts off corner, and as he looks up at Wullie he raises the segment between thumb and knife to his mouth.)*[57] Who?

---

[57]Alberta Theatre Projects used pieces of black licorice stuck together to form Malleable's chewing tobacco plug (Production Meeting, February 1977, Alberta Theatre Projects Archives, Alberta Theatre Projects Office).

Wullie: Old Cloutie.

Malleable: *(Getting the chew right.)* Who's he?

Pipe: You ought to know, Malleable. Old friend of yours.

Malleable: I don't know anybody by that name. Now there was a fellow—Coonie—Herb Coonie—lived just south of Cavan there—he curled—I remember once in a green bonspiel back in ...

Pipe: Cloutie. Old Nick ...

Wullie: Old Scratch. The Devil, Malleable.

Malleable: *(Goes on chewing a second—hitch in the rhythm.)* Oh— him. *(Spits in the stove.)*

Wullie: We have a match on Sunday night. I—uh—I have an agreement with him. A great deal depends on who wins the match.

Malleable: Oh?

Wullie: It's up to you whether you curl or not. Doesn't concern you—however it turns out. Just me.

Malleable: *(Ceases chewing suddenly.)* An' if we lose?

Wullie: If we lose—the Devil has one more MacCrimmon soul. I'd like to depend on you for third.

Malleable's mouth is ominously still as he considers the proposition.

Malleable: Why—*(One slow chew.)* sure, Wullie—*(Two slow chews.)* sure—*(Back in gear and chewing naturally.)*

Wullie: Thank you, Malleable.

Pipe: Now look, Malleable—about Clock ...

Malleable: Uh-huh. You tell Clock, you tell Father O'Halloran. I wouldn't say nothin' to Clock.

Wullie: Sunday night.

Malleable: Okay. Sunday night. *(He and Pipe-fitting are on their way out.)* Don't you worry none, Wullie.

Wullie: Aye-he. We better get in a couple of practices.

Malleable and Pipe: *Okay, Wullie. (They go out.)*

Wullie picks up the Devil's curling boots. We see that he gets an idea. He sits at the last to work on them as Reverend Pringle enters. This time Wullie wants to see him.

Wullie: Reverend Pringle.

Pringle: *(Holding out receipt.)* Sorry—meant to drop this into you sooner—your receipt—the new church. *(Annie Brown has entered the shop.)* You'll need it when you do your returns—charitable donation.

Wullie: *(Extraordinarily warm.)* Thank you—thank you, Reverend. Nice cup of coffee?

Pringle: No—I—*(Sees that Wullie wants to talk to him.)* oh—all right. Black—

Annie Brown enters.

Wullie: *(Goes around the counter for coffee pot. He has a mug in his hand. The Reverend has sat in a chair.)* I have a matter of some importance—Mrs. Brown.

Annie: Yes?

Wullie: Was there something? *(Pause.)* In the line of shoe repair? *(Pause.)* Harness?

Annie: No—no. I just saw Mr. Pringle come in and I have further to report on the corruption of our children in our schools.

Wullie: Some other time—some other place. I have a *private* matter to discuss with Mr. Pringle. *(Pause as Annie doesn't budge.)* Mrs. Brown—the back of your head would be a treat.

Annie: *(Stares at Wullie—she doesn't get it: "The back of your head would be a treat." It's like Chaucer: dialect, therefore a little difficult to understand.)* This is a serious matter.

Wullie: So's mine, and private. *(He "helps" her out but she will not go far, for we can see her outside, peering in the window.)* Now then, Reverend—a little more coffee?

Pringle: No—no—thanks. Ah—just what is this private matter?

Wullie: Oh—yes—*(This is pretty tough and Wullie isn't quite sure how best to begin.)* Yes—

Pringle: Serious matter?

Wullie: Mortally. *(He goes to the phone and dials, then:)* Clock? Clock—I'd like for you to drop over to my—it's

Wullie—you know any other MacCrimmons?—I'd like for you to drop over to my shop. Now, Clock, now—it is very important, more than your watch repairs—all right. *(He hangs up and turns to Pringle.)* There's to be a curling-match.

Pringle: When?

Wullie: Very soon. Maybe—too soon. A special curlin' ... *(He sees that Annie has face pressed up against the glass. He goes to it and yanks down the blind. He comes back to Pringle.)* I would appreciate it very much if you didna' say anything to anybody of what I am about to tell you. *(Pause.)* You remember a couple of weeks back we had a conversation—the day you put me down for twenty dollars for your new Methodist church?

Pringle: Yes—though it's United.

Wullie: This match—it's against—we're curling against the gentleman for whom I'm fixing a pair of curling boots. We—uh—spoke of him.

Pringle: What! You're not telling me—you aren't—now just a minute ...

Wullie: I and my rink curl Sunday night against the Devil and his rink from Hell.

Pringle: Have you gone out of your mind ...

Wullie: No—I have not. I made a bargain with him ...

Pringle: Look—if a curling match is that important to you, there's no need to cook up a wild excuse like that to ...

Wullie: It's no wild excuse, Mr. Pringle. I've told you just how it is.

Pringle: *(Laughing.)* All right—all right.

Wullie: *(Clears throat.)* I'd appreciate it very much if you didna' say anything to anybody—what I've just told you.

Pringle: Why—of course not—don't worry about that.

Wullie: How—how is the collection for the new church coming along?

Pringle: Fine—just fine.

Wullie: *(Crossing behind counter to his cash box.)* I—uh—I've been thinking it over. Ye may put me down for a bit more if you care to.

Pringle: Now that's very ...

Wullie: A hundred dollars more.

Pringle: Oh—you can't afford ...

Wullie: —an' while you're down here—you might drop in on Pipe-fitting Brown—

Pringle: I've already called on him.

Wullie: It'll do no harm to call on him again. You might tell him you've just seen me and I've upped my contribution. Tell him—uh—tell him considerin' what's at stake Sunday night it can do no harm. *(Pause.)* I think you'll find Pipe-fitting in a co-operative mood. *(Gives Pringle envelope containing one hundred dollars.)*

Pringle: *(Looking in envelope.)* But a hundred dollars—a hundred and twenty dollars—that hardly seems—it's a lot of money for—

Wullie: Had you attended the Old Country church I did as a boy, Mr. Pringle—had you heard a few of the sermons I did, you would think a hundred and twenty dollars little enough. Be sure to call on Pipe-fitting.

Pringle: I will. *(He exits and as he does so Clock Brown enters.)*

Clock: *(Crossing to stove.)* All right, Wullie—what was so important I had to come right over—an' me two weeks behind on watch repairs.

Annie, who we have seen outside, decides she can get more dope from Pringle and follows him off.

Wullie: *(Placing a copper rivet on the counter.)* I know it's a strange request, Clock. But it's an important one. I want it just like that, only silver.

Clock picks up the rivet and examines it carefully.

Clock: Looks like a rivet.

Wullie: It is a rivet.

Clock: Copper rivet.

Wullie: That's right.

Clock: You want me to make you up one just like it—only silver. Silver rivet?

Wullie: Aye-he.

Clock: Wouldn't be any trick at all to silverplate this one. Lot easier—a silver rivet would cost ...

Wullie: *(Tensely.)* Now look, Clock—you must get it right. Exactly right. I want a rivet—like that. Silver—solid silver—sterling silver. It must not be plated. A sterling-silver rivet.

Clock: Okay—okay I'll do it for you beginning the week.

Wullie: Beginning of the week's no good to me. It's no good at all. I must have it tomorrow morning.

Clock: Look—I never rush you on the boots. I'm a busy man like you are. I got the Husbay wedding—folks coming in buying china—cut glass—silver—I got way behind on my watch-repairing.

Manitoba Theatre Centre (1982):
Richard Vincent-Hurst as Clock; Wayne Robson as Wullie.

Wullie: Believe me, Clock—it's important.

Clock: *(Pause.)* All right. All right.

Wullie: Tomorrow by nine o'clock.

Clock: *(Exiting.)* All right.

Wullie looks after him, then crosses to have another look at the contract. He then picks up his coffee mug for a drink, but as he brings the mug to his lips the thought of coffee disgusts him. He empties the mug in a small trash can, reaches in one of his drawers and pulls out a Scotch bottle. He pours one hell of a lot of Scotch. Facing the audience, he lifts the mug:

Wullie: *(Fervently.)* Stand fast, Craigellachie[58]—*(He lifts the mug to his mouth and drinks long. He lowers it.)* And— curl to beat Hell.

There is a loud crash of thunder and the lights fade to black.

———— •••• ————

ACT II

The Jock McNair Memorial Rink.[59] Wullie, Pipe-fitting, and Malleable are on stage checking out and cleaning the ice. Clock enters. They all shake hands and exchange good lucks. Clock touches button[60] with right hand and crosses himself (like members of the Montreal Canadiens do before a game).

---

[58]Craigellachie is the name of a high rock in Morayshire, Scotland, where a beacon fire was lit to call the Clan Grant to battle during the clan wars. Their battle cry was "Stand fast, Craigellachie!"

[59]An inside joke—Rick McNair was the artistic director of Theatre Calgary when *Black Bonspiel* was first produced in 1979 and 1980.

[60]The one-foot white circle in the centre of the house (the target area) which consists of twelve-foot (blue), eight-foot (white), and four-foot (red) concentric circles.

Pipe: *(Seeing Clock.)* The old rugged cross, eh? Get it off your chest. "Homini Domini Bomini."[61]

In the distance the sound of bagpipes.

Clock: What the hell's that racket?

Pipe: Kiyoots.[62]

Clock: Kiyoots nothin'! Bagpipes!

Pipe: Funny thing about bagpipes. I can't tell which direction they're comin' from. *(They have been coming from underneath the stage.)* They seem to come at you from all directions at once.

Clock: Aren't these fellows awful fussy for a little pick-up game? *(He turns to Wullie.)* What's that tune, Wullie?

Wullie: 'Tis pibroch. The finest lament ever composed. *(Pause.)* "MacCrimmon Will Never Return." *(Sadly.)*

Pipe: Sure cheery.

There is a loud explosion, flash lightning, as the Devil's rink appears.[63]

Devil: *(Reading sign.)* "Jock McNair Memorial Rink." This must be it.

Bagpipes wail to a stop.

---

[61]Pipe is poking fun at the rituals and Latin prayers of the Catholic Church.

[62]Coyotes, as pronounced by Canadian foothills and prairie people (as opposed to the American "Ki-oat-ee").

[63]In the Alberta Theatre Projects production, the Devil's rink's curling rocks and brooms were flown in (lowered from above) in a second explosion of fire and smoke (Prompt Script, 1997, Alberta Theatre Projects Archives, Alberta Theatre Projects Office).

Theatre Calgary (1979): Michael Ball as the Devil.

Devil: Good evening, gentlemen.

Malleable, Pipe, and Wullie: *(Unenthusiastically.)* Evenin'—how's things—mmmh.

Devil: The visiting rink's all here. May I introduce my men— first my skip, Mr. Fawkes.

Wullie, Malleable, Clock, and Pipe: To meet you. Pleasure. Evening.

Guy: Evening.

Clock: *(Surprised at the other's reluctance to be hospitable, he takes the initiative.)* Evening. Just call me Clock.

Theatre Aquarius (1985): Dee R. McCafferty as Guy Fawkes; John Bayliss as the Devil; Gerald Lenton as Macbeth; Allen Stewart-Coates as Judas Iscariot.

Guy: Nice to meet you. Call me Guy.

Clock: Guy.

Devil: My second, Mr. Iscariot.

Malleable, Wullie, and Pipe: *(As before.)* Pleasure. Glad to know you. How do you do?

Clock: *(His surprise is turning to slight annoyance.)* Pleasure. I didn't quite get the name.

Judas: Iscariot, sir, and yours? *(Nervously he jingles change in his pocket.)*

Clock: Brown. Charlie Brown. Just call me Clock—so's you don't get me mixed up with Pipe-fitting and Malleable.

Devil: And my third. A dependable man with a guard rock.
Countryman of yours, Mr. MacCrimmon—Mr. Macbeth.
*(Seeing his boots that Wullie has brought with him and set
down on one of the benches.)* Now—my boots.

Wullie moves to give them to him but is interrupted by:

Macbeth: Tomorrow, and tomorrow, and tomorrow,
Curls in this petty pace from end to end,
To the last rock of recorded time;
And all our yesterdays have lighted fools
The way to icy death.

Wullie moves again but:

Macbeth: Out, out, brief candle!
Life's but a sweeping shadow, a poor curler
That slides crab-like his hour along the ice
And then he curls no more.

Wullie attempts a third time but:

Macbeth: It is a match
Played by an idiot, full of sound and fury,
(Devil glares at him.) Signifying nothing.[64]

---

[64]This is a close parody of Macbeth's famous soliloquy in *Macbeth*, V.v.17–27:
   Tomorrow, and tomorrow, and tomorrow,
   Creeps in this petty pace from day to day,
   To the last syllable of recorded time;
   And all our yesterdays have lighted fools
   The way to dusty death. Out, out, brief candle!
   Life's but a walking shadow, a poor player
   That struts and frets his hour upon the stage
   And then is heard no more. It is a tale
   Told by an idiot, full of sound and fury
   Signifying nothing.

Wullie: Your boots.

Devil: Beautiful.

Clock: Where'd you say you was from?

Macbeth: Fife, sir. There's one did laugh in his sleep and one cried "Murder." One cried "God bless us" and "Amen" the other.[65]

Clock: *(Beginning to dawn on him that there's something funny here.)* Say—what the hell's goin' on here!

Devil: Now—have you any preference as to the end of the rink to start ...

Pipe: Only one end to start from. Scoreboard's there.

Devil: As visiting rink would you mind indulging us— starting from the other end first?

Wullie: All right with us. I have no ... *(He breaks off to look with surprise ... Clock and Pipe-fitting look too.)*

Guy Fawkes (with plumed hat and slashed breeches) is walking down the rink with the scoreboard under his arm. We see him walk to the starting end of the rink, lift the scoreboard to a post, and begin hammering. We also see Judas and Macbeth sliding the rocks to the other end.

Malleable: *(Who had been busy putting on his overshoes, suddenly looks up.)* Hey ... What's he doing! Your skip ... why's he moved the scoreboard from the other end of the ice?

---

[65]Macbeth slips back to the moment just after he has murdered Duncan (*Macbeth*, II.ii.23–30).

Why'd he take the board down an' bring it to this end
and ...

Devil: Just a slight preparation before we start, gentlemen.

*Guy is stepping back from scoreboard, which he has nailed up. He
surveys his work. We see scoreboard, and that it's upside down.*

Clock: Startin' the wrong end of the ice! Turnin' the scoreboard upside down! I don't get it.

Guy: You soon will, mate.

*Clock stares after Fawkes as Pipe-fitting steps up and takes him by the
arm.*

Pipe: It's all right, Clock. It's all right.

Pipe-fitting has Clock by the sleeve—is trying to placate him.

Clock: Well, it isn't! That long, thin, hungry-looking fellow
with the red beard. One that turned the board around.
Somethin' funny about him.

Pipe: An Englishman, that's all ...

Clock: He didn't have any hammer when I shook hands with
him. An' his name ... uh ...

Pipe: Fox.

Clock: Yeah—Guy Fox—now that name seems kind of
familiar to me. The whole outfit seems funny to me.
You take that fellow from Fife—mutterin' all about
tomorrow an' tomorrow an' tomorrow ...

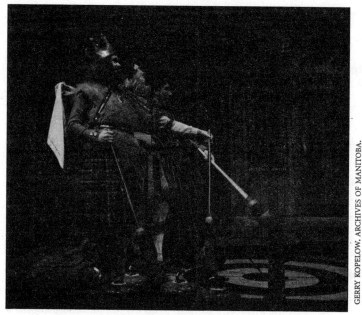

Manitoba Theatre Centre (1982): Brian Paul as Macbeth;
Robert MacDonald as Guy Fawkes; Peter Smith as Judas Iscariot.

Pipe: Farmer. Droughted out six years runnin'—no crop.
Kind of got him a bit. Sort of his way of sayin' next
year—next year—I'll get a forty-bushel crop next
year.[66]

Clock: Yeah? *(He's not convinced at all.)* That other fellow—
the visitin' second ... He ...

Pipe: He's all right, Clock.

---

[66]"Next year country" describes the prairies of the Depression years, whose farmers prayed
for better weather and crops "next year."

Clock: Always jinglin' silver in his pocket—what was his name?

Pipe: I didn't get it either, Clock. I think he's a cattle-buyer from out Olds way. They're just getting the coin ready to toss for first rock ... Malleable ...

Judas gives (reluctantly) a coin to Macbeth, who tosses it.

Malleable: ... Tails.

Devil: *(As the coin lands.)* You gentlemen first. We have the hammer.[67]

Clock: *(Picking up the coin.)* Let me see that coin. Hey—that's no Canadian quarter—hell, it isn't even American. Some kind of a Roman head on it. *(Malleable knocks it out of Clock's hand and it lands right in Judas's hand.)*

Wullie: Clock—curl your first rock. *(Clock looks down to Wullie—Wullie goes and gets his rock.)*

Wullie: Nice and easy—right in front.

Clock gets set and curls his first rock. Malleable and Pipe-fitting sweep.

Wullie: Nice rock, Clock.

Devil: *(From other end.)* We're looking for a takeout, Guy. Lots of weight.

Guy Fawkes sets himself to curl his first rock.

---

[67]The hammer is the last shot in each end, and the team that has the hammer has the advantage. Here, the Devil wins the coin toss at the beginning of the game and chooses to have Wullie's team throw the first rock so that he will have the hammer.

Clock: Hey—hold on a minute.

Guy pays no attention—curls his first rock.

Clock: That ain't right—he's skip—skips don't—*(Looking around wildly for someone to hear his protest.)* Skips don't curl first—skips got to curl last! Where's their— that fellah ... *(He stops with mouth open as he looks down the ice:)*

The Devil's men are sweeping madly—but in the wrong direction. They come from the opposite side of the stage to meet the rock from the far end. The sweepers are Macbeth and Iscariot, but now their long jumbo sweater coats and their curling tams have been replaced. Macbeth is in a kilt but with gold crown. Judas is in a long black robe with a cord belt.

Clock: Sweeping backwards! Skip first! Lead last! Scoreboard upside down! Judas! *(This stops Iscariot in his tracks as he was returning to the other end. Clock realizes what he has said. Judas flips a coin, chuckles, and moves off.)* Yeah! Judas Iscariot! A second name of Iscariot! The visitin' rink's from Hell, boys! *(All out in sheer terror.)* You're riskin' your immortal souls in a Black Bonspiel!

Wullie: *(Entering from other end of rink.)* It's all right, Clock— all right! You're curling on the right rink, Clock.

Clock: All right for you Protestants. But there ain't any rink a right rink in this sort of a match! *(Panic shows on his face as he throws down his broom.)* I wouldn't curl another rock ...

Pipe: Wullie's got an understanding with the visitin' head, Clock.

Clock: *(Turning on Pipe-fitting.)* You said his second was a cattle-buyer from Olds.

Pipe: *(All are watching and listening.)* Pull yourself together an' get your next rock—it's just Wullie he's interested in—nothin' to do with the rest of us.

Clock: How can you! How can you be sure it's only Wullie ...

Pipe: Look, Clock—you're in the same boat as me—you got nothin' to lose in the first place.

The Devil listens to this exchange with lifted eyebrows. He smiles and inclines his head slightly to Clock.

Devil: That's right. Quite right, Mr. Brown.

Clock: *(Instant anger. "Got me in the bag, has he!")* Is that so. Is that—so! Gimme that there rock! All right ... *(He looks down the ice, set to curl.)* What you want Wullie?

Wullie: *(Calling back to him.)* Take it out, Clock—take it out.

Clock, toe in the hack,[68] kneels—arm comes back slowly, then forward to release the rock. His face has grim determination and a grimace almost of pain as he releases the rock. Pipe-fitting and Malleable sweep furiously in front of the rock. Two-thirds of the way they stop and stare anxiously as the rock pursues its way ... we hear the lambasting crack of Clock's rock as it strikes Fawkes's.

Devil: Nice rock, Mr. Brown.

---

[68] Rubber foothold in the ice on which the curler places his foot so that he can push off and slide his rock down the ice.

Clock: *(Contemptuously.)* Better'n a kick in the ass with a frozen boot.

We are now in another part of town.

Mr. Pringle comes on but stops as:

Annie: *(Off.)* Mr. Pringle—Mr. Pringle!

Annie enters.

Annie: *(A little short of breath, catching up to him.)* The rink—the curling rink! They've snuck over to the outdoor rink. They are curling! I got home from church and Charlie was gone! His broom was gone—his coat was gone—his tam was gone! *(Wildly.)* And I knew right away—I knew—they've got a sneak curling match on Sunday! *(Pause.)* Well?

Pringle: Well what?

Annie: Aren't you going to stop it?

Pringle: The by-law hasn't been voted on yet.

Annie: But it's against the Lord's Day Act! It's breaking His sixth commandment.

Pringle: Fourth.

Annie: So! That Wullie MacCrimmon ...

Pringle: Already been broken—we can't put it back together again, can we Mrs. Brown?

Annie: We can stop them!

Pringle: I don't know ...

Annie: I do. This wicked Sabbath curling—and my Charlie with his back ... After this he's not curling again! If Wullie MacCrimmon ... not on any night of the week! Lower lumbar region—Charlie has a disc that goes out when he just sneezes ...

We hear the faint sound of bagpipes.

Annie: My goodness! Bagpipes. It's not just a pick-up match ... Bagpipes—that means they're running a whole bonspiel—a Sunday bonspiel ...

Pringle: You're right—They've gone too far—Come on!

They move off.

Lights back up in the curling-rink. We see Wullie and Pipe-fitting at the downstage bench. The Devil walks past them. The scoreboard reads four to two for the visiting rink.

Devil: **(To Wullie.)** Lovely—nice snug fit! *(He is very pleased with himself and with the score.)* I don't know when I've had a more comfortable pair of curling boots. Thanks to you. *(He moves off.)*

Pipe: Only got four ends to go, Wullie.

Wullie: *(Looking after the Devil.)* Aach! Confound him. *(Turns back to Pipe-fitting.)* Only silver can confound the Devil.[69] Did you know that, Pipe-fitting?

---

[69]In folklore, the silver bullet or knife was believed to be the only effective weapon against various evil figures such as vampires, witches, and werewolves.

Neptune Theatre (1986): Maxim Mazumdar as the Devil.

Pipe: No ... I didn't.

Wullie: It's true.

We see Macbeth curl a rock. Judas and Guy Fawkes come on sweeping again backwards. Then all three cross to the other end.

Devil: Nice rock, Mac.

Pipe: (*Anxiously.*) Is Malleable's back holdin' out all right?

Wullie: Aye. An' it will ... an' we will.

Pipe: Wullie ... I was rememberin' ... that Three Hills Bonspiel year before last ...

Wullie: No!

Pipe: When the Consort rink come from way behind ...

Wullie: No ...

Pipe: ... just a touch of corn syrup on the bottom the skip's
rock ... Hell, anything goes agin' the Devil. *(Wullie
emphatically shakes his head.)* All right ... but there's
nothin' to stop us razzin' 'em ... put 'em off of their
stride ... rattle 'em ...

Wullie: Devil does not rattle easy.

Pipe: Oh ... not him. I'd pick that sissy English fellah in them
coloured bloomers—feather in his tam ... I figger it
wouldn't be too hard to get him to blow up.[70]

Wullie: I'm not so sure.

Pipe: Judas then.

Wullie: Macbeth.

Pipe: Why him?

Wullie: He's an ambitious man—though he was not much of a
self-starter—and he's curling third—get it?

Pipe: No.

---

[70]In the Alberta Theatre Projects production which replaced Guy Fawkes with Lizzie
Borden, Pipe's lines become, "I'd pick the uppity American lady with the sunny outfit ... I
figger it wouldn't be too hard to get her to fall to pieces" (Prompt Script, 1997, Alberta
Theatre Projects Archives, Alberta Theatre Projects Office). "Pieces" plays on the school-
yard skipping song: "Lizzie Borden took an axe / And gave her mother forty whacks. / And
when she saw what she had done, / She gave her father forty-one."

Wullie: If they were to win this match—then I'd end up on the
                 Devil's rink ... What does he want me to curl?

Pipe: Yeah! Third! You'd bump him!

Wullie: That's right.

Devil: Let's get on with the match, Mr. MacCrimmon.

*Wullie and the Devil go off to the other end of the rink. Pipe-fitting and
Clock set to sweep Malleable's rock.*

Clock: C'mon, Pipe.

Malleable: Where do you want it, Wullie?

Wullie: In turn,[71] Malleable.

Annie: *(Off.)* Stop it—stop it! That's it!

Annie and Pringle enter.

Annie: *(Crossing to Malleable.)* Sneaking off to curl on Sunday.

*Malleable, who was about to curl his rock, takes Annie by the shoulders
and moves her off the ice.*

Annie: Charlie!

Malleable curls his rock. Clock and Pipe-fitting sweep off.

---

[71]As the curler delivers a rock he can turn the handle in or out so that the rock's rotation
will cause it to curve right or left as it slides down the ice. Here Wullie asks Malleable to
rotate his rock clockwise.

Theatre Aquarius (1993): Richard Binsley as Malleable; Helen Beavis
as Annie Brown; David Mallis as Clock; Roger Dun as Pipe.

Wullie: *(Off.)* Don't never leave it! Don't never leave it! Right
on the button, Malleable.

Pringle steps onto the ice.

Pringle: Hold it! Hold it! Wullie—Wullie.

Wullie: *(Coming to Pringle.)* Please, Mr. Pringle.

Pringle: This match is contrary to the Lord's Day Alliance
Act[72]—

---

[72]The federal Lord's Day Act, 1906, prohibited sports, entertainment, and most business on
Sundays. In 1982, as a result of the new Canadian Charter of Rights and Freedoms, the
Lord's Day Act was successfully challenged and revoked.

Wullie: This is the most important match of my life—

Pringle: Couldn't you—call it off—move it ahead a day? Wait till midnight?

Devil: *(Has come up to them.)* If he does—he forfeits!

Wullie: I canna'—I willna'!

Pringle: Oh come on—a few hours—a day—another evening!

Devil: Forfeit!

Wullie: I made a bargain. I must keep it! To the letter!

Pringle: I always thought you were on the side of law and order.

Wullie: I try to be. This is special.

Pringle: How?

Wullie can't tell him. He shakes his head, turns to the Devil.

Wullie: Curl your rock—I'll not forfeit!

Annie: No, Charlie—no! That's your last end, Charlie.

Malleable: Leave me alone—I got a match to curl!

As Malleable comes by the Devil, the Devil deliberately and blatantly sticks out a hoof. Malleable does the flying pratfall of all time. Pringle and Annie run to him exclaiming. They bend down, but Malleable remains curled on the ice in the fetal position.

Annie: Your back! Your disc!

Pringle: *(Pointing to Devil.)* You tripped him! *(Devil shrugs and shakes his head.)* You did! I saw you do it!

Wullie: *(Has come down the ice.)* Malleable, Malleable, you all right?

Clock: You okay, Malleable?

Wullie: How's your back, Malleable?

Malleable: *(Groaning.)* She's out!

Pringle: He tripped him.

Devil: Let's get on with the match, gentlemen.

Wullie: My third's in agony!

All work to get Malleable to the bench, which is upstage.

Pringle: Wullie—that man tripped him—I saw it!

Wullie: Aye-he. He has a bad name for not playing fair.

Pipe: What we gonna do, Wullie—Malleable can't curl.

Devil: Forfeit?

Pringle: *(Pause.)* No—I'll curl third for you.

Annie: Reverend Pringle! It's Sunday!

Pringle: Not anymore it isn't.

Annie: But it's ...

Pringle: Three minutes past midnight.

Annie: No, past eleven.

Pringle: Daylight saving.

Annie: We're not on daylight saving.

Pringle: God is.

Annie: Reverend Pringle!

Pringle: For tonight. Now, Annie, you get that poor man home. *(Moving down to the bench downstage, he removes his coat.)* Wullie, Clock, Pipe-fitting. *(They come over to him.)* I'll curl third for you, but there are certain conditions. Wullie, I want to see you in church next Sunday morning. *(Pause, then Wullie reluctantly agrees.)* And Wullie, I want your support.

Wullie: Support—wi' what?

Pringle: The anti–Sabbath-curling by-law.

Wullie: Oh no!

Pringle: All right—no deal—go ahead—forfeit the match!

Wullie is trapped. He looks at the Devil, who smiles. Wullie makes up his mind.

Wullie: Lesser of two evils! Let's curl!

Devil: Forfeit.

Wullie: No! The Reverend's curling third for me.

Devil: *(He has taken out his contract with Wullie. He holds it up.)* Section Four—Paragraph 2A—"If the Party of the first part or the Party of the second part, for any reason other than those exceptions listed in addenda IIIC and IV, do not finish the regulation eight ends and/or extra ends—they shall forfeit!"

Pringle: *(Reaching for the contract.)* Let me see that!

Devil: Private agreement, Reverend, between me and Mr. MacCrimmon.

Wullie: *(He has taken out his copy of the agreement and crossed to the Devil. Meanwhile, Malleable and Pipe-fitting have pulled Pringle away.)* Oh yes—just as I thought. Nowhere—nowhere at all in that Agreement for Sale is there a No-Substitution Clause.

Neptune Theatre (1986): Bill Carr as Pipe; Maxim Mazumdar as the Devil; Joseph Rutten as Malleable; Don Harron as Wullie; Kelly Handerek as Clock; Glenn White as Reverend Pringle.

Devil: There is no clause saying you can substitute!

Wullie: Nor is there one sayin' I can *not* substitute. So if you refuse my new third—on no grounds for refusal—then you forfeit.

Devil: *(Crossing to the rest of his rink, stage left.)* Match over—I'm taking my rink off the ice!

Wullie: Forfeit!

Pringle: A man can get a bad name by not keeping agreements. *(The Devil glares at him.)* And—cheating—by tripping!

Clock: Are we curlin' this match or aren't we curlin'—

Guy: *(To the Devil.)* Why not? Church has traditionally been on the losing side. I should know.[73]

Devil: All right. All right! *(And he gets set to curl his rock. Clock and Pipe-fitting go upstage. All others go off, except for the Devil, who is going to curl. He does so, and as Guy and Judas come on sweeping—backwards—the lights fade to black.)*

We are now in another part of town.

With Annie helping him—his hand clutching and bracing his back—Malleable enters.

Annie: Easy, Charlie—you see—

Malleable groans.

---

[73]That is, in struggles for power the Church generally loses to the State. Fawkes, a Catholic revolutionary, was hanged, drawn, and quartered by the State for treason.

Annie: God's punishment.

Malleable groans.

Annie: Get you home—heating pad on it—still have to run its course. I think there are still some of those muscle-relaxant pills from the last time. *(They have stopped mainly because Malleable has simply decided not to take another step in the direction they're going.)* Now come on, Charlie. *(She applies a gentle encouragement with her arm.)*

Malleable: Aye-yeigh!

Annie: Oh!

Malleable: Take your arm away!

Annie: I'm only trying to help!

Malleable: Don't *(Grabs back at a new spasm.)* touch me!

Annie: *(She drops her arm and steps back.)* You'll never make home without my ...

Malleable: That's right! *(He is now like one of those mechanical dock figures jerkily and painfully making a 180-degree turn.)* That's right—I'm—not—going to make it—home.

Annie: Charlie!

Malleable: But I am going to make it back to the curling rink to see how Wullie and Clock and Pipe-fitting and the Reverend Pringle make out in that curlin' match!

Annie: If you don't come home with me right now I will never speak to you again!

Malleable slowly turns out to the audience and smiles.[74]

Lights back up on the curling rink. We see Wullie and the Devil stage right. Malleable is sitting on one of the upstage benches. Macbeth is on the other. The scoreboard reads seven to four.

Devil: Seven to four, Mr. MacCrimmon. I had expected a better match from your rink.

Wullie: Aye-he.

Devil: Last end, only six rocks to go—three is a pretty healthy lead.

Wullie: Aye-he.

Devil: If—ah—you'd care to concede ...

Wullie: We're conceding nothin'!

Devil: I'd be willing to—I wouldn't hold you to the second contract.

Wullie: I'll keep my bargain. If you win, I'll curl for you at no cost. *(He looks up at the Devil. Wullie's mouth tightens with determination.)* But Mr. Cloutie, don't count your souls before they're hatched.

---

[74]Mitchell approved the addition of this stage direction and Annie's last speech in the 1980 Lennoxville Festival and 1982 Manitoba Theatre Centre productions of the play. The director, Rick McNair, persuaded Mitchell that they give "a great button to the scene" (email to Orm Mitchell from Rick McNair, June 5, 2004).

The Devil has quiet and satisfied amusement on his face. He lifts his eyebrows and shrugs. So be it.

Wullie prepares to direct Pringle's second rock as third.

Wullie: In turn, Reverend.

Pringle, offstage, curls his rock, and Clock and Pipe-fitting sweep it in. They beam as it looks to be a good rock.

Pipe: That's more like it, Reverend. We're counting two now.

Devil: Never win a bonspiel on bald ends.[75]

Malleable: Ain't gonna be bald-headed this last end. You wait an' see. *(And in his excitement he gets another spasm. The Devil smiles. Pipe-fitting has gone over to Macbeth, who is still sitting on bench.)*

Pipe: Hey—Macbeth ...

Macbeth: I have no spur to prick the sides of my intent, but only vaulting ambition ...[76]

Pipe: Yeah ... Wullie told me ... did you ever stop to think you got a lot ridin' on this match ...

Macbeth: Macbeth hath murdered sleep ...

Pipe: See ... if you was to win this match ... Wullie comes on your rink ... an' if he comes onto your rink—he's gonna curl third ... an' if he curls third ...

---

[75]In a bald or blank end no scoring rocks remain in the house. The Devil has the last rock in this final end, and he is certain that he can take out all of Wullie's scoring rocks.
[76]From *Macbeth*, I.vii.25–27.

Manitoba Theatre Centre (1982): Brian Paul as Macbeth;
Andrew Gillies as Pipe.

Macbeth: Macbeth shall sweep no more ...[77]

Pipe: Yeah—that's right—but if we was to win this match ...

But Macbeth is not even listening to Pipe-fitting. Indeed, he is acting quite strangely as he puts out and down his hand.

Macbeth: Is this a curling rock I see before me,
The handle toward my hand?[78]
I have thee not *(Looks down to the ice.)* and yet I see
thee still.
Art thou not, granite stone, sensible to sweeping
As to sight? Or art thou but

---

[77]Alberta Theatre Projects adds stage direction, "*drops broom*" (Prompt Script, 1997, Alberta Theatre Projects Archives, Alberta Theatre Projects Office). Macbeth in this and the previous speech echoes *Macbeth*, II.ii.36–44.

[78]Manitoba Theatre Centre adds a line here: "Come, let me clutch thee" (Prompt Script, 1981–82, P 4439, file 16, Archives of Manitoba).

A curling rock of the mind, a false creation,
Out-turning from the heat-oppressed brain?
I see thee yet, in form as palpable ...
(*Seeing the rock Pringle has just curled and reaching
for it.*)
As this ...[79]

Pipe: Hey—no—no. We're curling from that end over there.

Devil: (*Leading him off left.*) That was beautiful, Mac.
(*Macbeth is still reaching for an imaginary stone.*) No—
no—the real one's over there!

Pipe: (*Anxiously.*) What you think, Wullie?

Wullie: I think you got to him.

Pipe: Yeah—but four to seven. Can we do her, Wullie?

Wullie: All we can do is curl, Pipe-fitting. I don't understand it.
It's not working out. Not working out at all.

Pipe: What's not working out?

Wullie: (*Not letting the Devil, who has returned, hear.*) I had a
wee trick, but it's not working out. I doubt it can with

---

[79]This is a close parody of Macbeth's speech in *Macbeth*, II.i.33–40:
   Is this a dagger which I see before me,
   The handle toward my hand? Come, let me clutch thee.
   I have thee not, and yet I see thee still,
   Art thou not, fatal vision, sensible
   To feeling as to sight? or art thou but
   A dagger of the mind, a false creation,
   Proceeding from the heat-oppress'd brain?
   I see thee yet, in form as palpable
   As this ...

only five more rocks to curl and four to catch up. *(Pause.)* I doubt it can.

Devil: Straight-handle takeout, Macbeth! And start thinking positively for a change.

Macbeth: ... which now I curl!

Macbeth curls from offstage as Judas and Guy sweep in other direction.

Devil comments on quality of rock thrown.

Pringle has come down the ice to hold broom for Wullie.

Pringle: What's it going to be, Wullie?

Wullie: I think I can clear that last rock out and leave us counting three.

Wullie goes off to curl his rock. Pringle looks suspiciously at the Devil. Wullie's rock comes on with Pipe-fitting and Clock sweeping. It's, naturally, a good rock.

Pipe: We're counting three now and they've only got two rocks left.

Devil: All right, Mac! Come here. Stand there. Hold your broom there. Don't move it!

As he walks offstage he starts to limp. He is puzzled. He does not understand where the pain is coming from. He goes off to curl his rock. Judas and Guy come on to sweep. The Devil's rock goes shooting down the ice. It goes right through the house. Wullie's rink is jubilant. Wullie shows Pringle where to set the broom, and as he and Clock and Pipe-fitting cross left:

Wullie: I think we have this one, boys, we have Old Cloutie by the tail on a downhill pull.

Wullie curls his rock. It comes right on target.

Pipe: We are counting four. That would make it eight to seven. The Devil has just got to blow his last rock.

Devil: *(Showing Mac where to hold broom.)* All right, Mac, I'm going to do a double takeout.

Macbeth: Double?

Devil nods his head.

Macbeth: Double ... toil and trou—*(But he gets no further as the Devil glares at him.)*[80]

The Devil crosses off left. He is in great agony. Barely able to walk.

Pringle: That gentleman seems to have something bothering him, wouldn't you say, Wullie?

Wullie: Maybe so, maybe so.

The Devil curls his last rock. It does not even make it past the hog line.

Malleable: Did you see that ... he hogged his rock.

Pringle: He hogged his last rock.

Pipe: We win by one point!

---

[80]Echoes the refrain to the three witches' song in *Macbeth*, IV.i.10: "Double, double toil and trouble, / Fire burn, and cauldron bubble."

Malleable, Pringle, and Pipe: Hogged his rock! Not worth a whoop. We count—we count. Devil blew up. We win by one rock. Match is over. *(All this accompanied by cheers and whoops.)*

Wullie: *(Moving downstage and banging his broom on the bench.)* We nailed his hide to a fence post.

Devil: *(Entering with a lopsided gait, for he is holding out one curling-boot.)* All right, MacCrimmon! This boot you resoled, you put a sharpened rivet between the inner and outer sole!

Wullie: Aye-he.

Devil: A sterling rivet ... to which I am allergic!

Wullie: I've heard tell. Any time you want your boots fixed, I'll do them free of charge.

Devil: Why you ...

There is a lambasting explosion of sound and lightning and smoke as the Devil and his rink vanish. As the smoke clears, the Reverend bends down and picks up the Devil's curling-boot. He turns to Wullie.

Pringle: He's a poor loser.

Wullie: Who?

Pringle: Ah ... the ... gentleman who just left.

Wullie: What ... gentleman?

Pipe: His own fault. He'd of had her in the bag if he hadn't blown up himself.

Wullie: Aye—he. His own fault. His feet.

Pipe: His feet?

Wullie: A man cannot curl a fine knockout match with his mind on his feet.

Pipe: Damn right. 'Xcuse me, Reverend.

Wullie: That wee trick I mentioned ... Ah, perhaps some time ... Reverend Pringle might explain it to you ... it's more in his line. *(Indicating boot.)* I'd like for you to have that, Reverend. Might help you put some bones in your sermon next Sunday.

Pringle: All right, Wullie.

Wullie: Pipe-fitting ... I'll be wanting you ... and Malleable and Clock to curl for me ... soon.

Pipe: Return match?

Wullie: Macdonald Brier. It's in the bag. *(Indicating agreement.)* Pipe-fitting—how old a man are you?

Pipe: Fifty-two.

Wullie: Ever heard of the Celestial Brier Playoffs?

Pipe: No ... I ain't.

Wullie: You'll curl second for me in that ... when your time comes.

Pipe: If she's what I think she is, Wullie ... that's one I kind of think I'll be curling agin you.

Pringle: Wullie ... If there's ever a return match with that
gentleman, I'd give anything to curl on your rink.

Wullie: Then you'll have to forget your by-law. He only curls
on the Sabbath.

Lights fade to black.

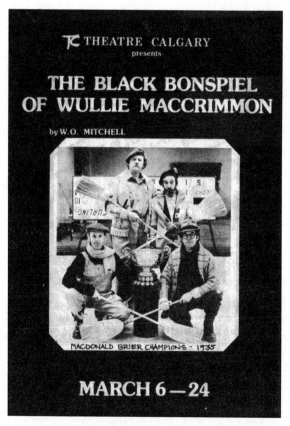

Theatre Calgary program cover (1979):
The Macdonald Brier "in the bag."

THE DEVIL'S INSTRUMENT

———✦✦✦———

INTRODUCTION BY W.O. MITCHELL

In the Gran Chaco of Paraguay, as well as in Uruguay, on the prairies and in the foothills of both Canada and the United States are the communal societies of the followers of Jacob Hutter. Since the Reformation[1] they have preserved their faith and their simple lifestyle. They even survived a massacre in Russia, which reduced them to fifteen souls, from whom all of today's Hutterites are descended. A genetic gift of practicality must have a great deal to do with their survival. Wherever they are, all Hutterites dress as they did centuries ago, sing the same Gregorian hymns, emulate Christ's apostles, resist worldliness, and obey the stern old men commonly called "the Bosses" in their patriarchal societies. From colony to colony little is different beyond individual preference for jacket fasteners: dome or button or hook-and-eye. Beards and dress and religious practice and prosperity and gentleness have made them

---

[1]Sixteenth-century movement, led by Martin Luther, for reform of the abuses of the Catholic Church which led to the establishment of the Reformed and Protestant Churches (OED).

ideal scapegoats. After the Atomic Holocaust God will probably still hold them as his hole card with which to win the human game all over again.

"A mouth organ is the devil's instrument," a Hutterite boy once told me in a café in the foothills many years ago. This was so, he said, because the love of it would diminish his love of God. Conformity in a puritan society is as much a problem for Jacob Schunk as it has been for other artists since long before the Reformation.

⊷⊶

CAST OF CHARACTERS

Jacob Schunk: A sixteen-year-old Hutterite boy who has lived with his grand-uncle ever since the death of his father and mother in a highway accident when he was four. Not long after that he lost an older brother, who left the colony. This does not mean that Jacob has only his grand-uncle for family. The colony itself is his family.

Darius Schunk: Jacob's much older brother, who left the colony to become a teacher and returned only to be excommunicated[2] because of the worldly ways he'd learned. Jacob hardly remembers Darius, for it is ten years since that shameful thing happened.

Marta Schreiber: A sixteen-year-old girl, who seems to Jacob the most beautiful girl in the colony, and therefore the world.

Peter, the Goose Boss: Jacob's grand-uncle. To be a Goose Boss is not nearly so important as to be a Cattle Boss or an Egg Boss. A

---

[2]In general terms, excommunication means to expel a member from the church. In Darius's case, because Hutterite colony life and church life are virtually one and the same, he is exiled from both church and community.

serious transgression of Peter's past may have made up God's mind that Peter should be only a Goose Boss.[3]

The Preacher: Actually the most powerful man in the colony; boss over all the bosses.

Vogel Unger: A boy of great faith, who may even overcome the handicap of his lisp to become a preacher when he grows up.

Marta's mother

John the Blacksmith: Marta's father.

Bone-setter

Oats and Barley Boss

Susan, Rachel, Ruth, Anna, Old woman, Woman one: Hutterite women.

Mike and Otto: Hutterite men.

Joe and Jake: Two truck drivers.

Wong: Palm Café proprietor.

Trucker

---

[3]Since its beginnings in the puritan reformation, patriarchy and hierarchy have been very strong elements in Hutterite society.

Scene 1

The interior of the Palm Café is filled with the loud sadness of "The Red River Valley"[4] coming from the old jukebox left stage, where Jacob Schunk stands listening while he waits for his grandfather, Peter, to be finished at the dentist's next door. Jacob is rapt in the music and is unaware of Wong behind the counter left stage. Wong lifts a swatter high and brings it down on the counter top. He misses and his eyes lift and circle to follow the fly, which evidently lights on the other side. Wong tries again. Another miss. Annoyed, he looks across at Jacob. He rounds the end of the counter and comes up behind Jacob. He taps him on the shoulder with the fly swatter.

Wong: *(As Jacob starts guiltily.)* What you want? You want buyee something. You buyee ... ha![5]

Jacob: Nothing, thank ...

Wong: Doesn't pay me some kinda money ... Listen my juice box ...

Jacob: I do not want to buy anything, thank you.

Wong: You kinda peopoh nevah buyee nothing ... nevah buyee dinnah ... ham egg ...

---

[4]Folk song made popular in the 1930s by Sons of the Pioneers (founded by Roy Rogers).
[5]Mitchell, like Mark Twain, prided himself on accurately capturing dialect in his characters' dialogue. The actor who plays Wong has to be very careful to mimic the speech patterns of a first-generation Chinese immigrant in a way that does not slip into racist caricature.

Two truckers, Joe and Jake, are presenting their bill at the counter.

Joe: Costs money. Hooterites too tight to spend.

Wong: *(Jabbing at cash register viciously.)* Nevah buyee ...
nevah buyee ... ice cream ... vanillah ... mapo wa'nut ...
nevah smoke ...

Jacob: Sinful. They ain't s'posed to smoke. Them bosses ...

Wong: ... Nevah buyee plug ... seegah ... you like plug?

Jacob: Nothing ... I would like only to ...

Wong: *(Shoving chewing tobacco plug across counter.)* You like
plug ... Black Judas ... you chew some ...

Jacob: I would only like to listen to the music out of the little
box.

Wong: *(Slapping Joe's change down on the counter with disgust.)*
You like music. Make music. Make you own.

Joe: He ain't even s'posed to whistle.

Wong: Make you own. Mouth ohgan. I got lots mouth ohgan.
You buyee one ... make you own music ... make religion
music.

Joe: Send him straight to hell, blowin' a mouth organ.
Better watch out, young fellow, one of them beardy
bosses comes in an' catches you listenin' to that juke
box ...

Jake: Aw, let him alone. Here ... *(Holds out a nickel.)* Have one on me, kid ... *(As Jacob hesitates.)* Go on ... stick it in the slot. Push that there lever down ...

Jacob: No thank ...

Jake: Come on ... it won't hurt you. Any the bosses show up I'll give you the high sign. They're all over in the Royal Beer Parlour suckin' down beer ...

Joe: You folks so religious ... won't smoke ... drink tea ... coffee ... chew ... when she comes to beer ... look out.

Jake: Stick that nickel in.

Jacob: No thank you.

Jake: What's wrong? *(Shoving the nickel at Jacob)* Here! First time I ever saw one of you people didn't ...

Jacob: No ... thank you ... I don't ...

Jake: ... jump at the chance a gettin' somethin' ...

Jacob: Please ... no.

Jake: Take it!

Darius has come up during this.

Darius: If he doesn't want to, he doesn't have to!

Jake: Who the ... I ain't tryin' to force nothin' on him ... I just ...

Darius: He doesn't want it ... obviously.

Jake: I just offered him a nickel for that jukebox an' he ...

Darius: He's told you at least three times ... he doesn't want it.

Jake: (*Shrugs and swings away.*) No skin off my ...

Wong: Alla time Hooterite come in ... nevah buyee ...

Darius: (*To Jacob.*) Don't let it ...

Wong: Nevah buyee ... nevah buyee even comb ...

Joe: Too tight.

Wong: Ice cream comb. All he do ... listen my juice box on othah peopoh nickoh ...

Jake: Then when you offer him a nickel to play ...

Jacob: Excuse me ... I will go away outside now.

Darius: No ... No. Sit down. Will you have a dish of ice cream with me?

Jake: Ain't gonna listen to music on my nickel ... sure as hell ain't gonna eat ice cream from a teetotal stranger.

Darius: Will you ... please?

Jake: He's gonna disappoint you, stranger.

Jacob: Thank you.

Jake: Well, I'll be ...

Darius:	Thank you. *(As they move towards the booths.)* What kind? Pink? Vanilla? Chocolate?
Jake:	Look at that, will you. Hooterite for you.
Joe:	Contrary.
Jake:	Touchy as a cut calf ... won't take my nickel ... some stranger from outa town, he ...

They go.

Jacob:	Pink.
Darius:	Pink.
Wong:	Pink.
Darius:	You ... you from the hook-and-eye ... the Cash River colony?
Jacob:	Yes.
Darius:	What is your name?
Jacob:	Jacob. Jacob Schunk.
Darius:	Jacob! Jacob Schunk!

Wong arrives with two dishes of ice cream.

Darius:	Jacob Schunk!
Wong:	Pink. Thirty cen'.

Darius: Oh ... yes ... yes ... thank you. *(Wong goes.)* Jacob Schunk. Your father ... your mother ... they live in the colony?

Jacob: My father and mother are dead.

Darius: Who looks after you?

Jacob: I work and I sleep with Peter, the Goose Boss. He is my grand-uncle.

Darius: Goose Boss! Isn't that women's work?

Jacob: *(With some spirit.)* No, it is not! It is important!

Darius: And ... will you be Goose Boss when you get older? *(Jacob works on the ice cream.)* I should think it would be much finer to be a Horse Boss or the Oats and Barley Boss ... or ...

Jacob: I would like to be a Goose Boss when I get older.

Darius: How old are you, Jacob?

Jacob: Sixteen.

Darius: I see. Then you do not go to school anymore?

Jacob: No.

Darius: For it was from the tree of knowledge that the apple came for Adam and Eve's first sin ... I know.

Jacob: Where are your father and mother?

Darius: Mine? *(Pause.)* They are dead. Like yours.

Jacob: And have you any sisters?

Darius: One brother.

Jacob: How old is he?

Darius: He is your age, Jacob.

Jacob: (*Suddenly.*) Is it hard to blow music out of a little mouth organ?

Darius: Do you like music?

Jacob: Oh yes! No! I don't know how to say it. It ... hurts me.

Darius: Hurts you!

Jacob: But not bad. It ... I ...

Darius: How does it ... hurt?

Jacob: Like when I come home ... when the hills are dark ... only high on top there is light there yet, and I see that die ... and it leaves me like ... like ...

Darius: Sad ... Jacob.

Jacob: Like I am the only one left in the whole world. It is like I am left hanging. And it hurts ... in your throat. I want to ... to cry, for something is lifting up in me, and I want to cry.

Darius: Is it the same with music?

Jacob: I think so ... the feeling. When you want something so you ache and it hurts ...

Darius: And you know it's sinful.

Jacob: Yes! Yes! It is the Devil's music! It ... *(Suddenly realizing the importance of what he has said and making a noble effort.)* I do not love ... like ... anything of the devil.

Darius: How do you know it is the devil's music? How can you know it isn't ...

Jacob: I know.

Darius: Because the bosses tell you? Because old men with their ...

Jacob: I know.

Darius: ... dry old hearts ... their very ordinary hearts ...

Jacob: I know it with my own heart.

Darius: ... their gross materialistic hearts ... tell you it is sinful?

Jacob: It is wicked and sinful!

Darius: Do you think the Devil likes beauty?

Jacob: It would send me to everlasting burning.

Darius: Jacob, that is not true.

Jacob: I know.

Darius: It is not true!

Jacob: The Preacher says it is true. The Chicken Boss says it is true. Otto, the Oats and Barley Boss ... He is head boss over all the bosses. He is just like Moses.

Darius: Is he?

Jacob: Yes. His beard is black and he is not afraid of anything. He is not afraid to look into the face of the Lord. He is not afraid.

Darius: Is he not?

Jacob: John the Blacksmith ... when I was a child, I used to think he looked like Christ. His beard is lovely. It is soft. His eyes are blue ... and Marta's ...

Darius: Marta's?

Jacob: He is Marta's father ... Marta Schreiber. Her eyes ... they are blue too.

Darius: Are they now?

Jacob: Yes. They are blue ... like a crocus is blue. The little braids, they ... do you know something?

Darius: What, Jacob?

Jacob: If you had a beard, then ... then you would look a lot like John the Blacksmith. *(Rises suddenly.)* Thank you for the ice cream.

Darius: That is nothing. *(Stopping him.)* Wait. About this ... mouth organ.

Jacob: No thanks. I am going to be a good boy like Vogel Unger.

Darius: Is he a good boy?

Jacob: Oh yes. He is going to be the Preacher when he ... *(He sits down again.)* He has faith.

Darius: Has he?

Jacob: He has tested it. He tested it two years ago, when he was shingling the new horse barn. He laid down his shingling hatchet and he told me he said to himself when the noon bell rang for dinner: "Our Christ walked upon the waters. Why not Vogel Unger, son of the Pig Boss?" Do you know what he did?

Darius: No, Jacob.

Jacob: The peak of the new horse barn is seventy-five feet up in the air. That is high.

Darius: That is high.

Jacob: Vogel Unger walked off it on to the air.

Darius: To test his faith.

Jacob: He told me he started walking towards the kitchen behind the spinning building where the women work.

Darius: I don't imagine he reached it, Jacob.

Jacob: *(Slowly shakes his head.)* No. The air did not hold him up. He fell fifty feet and onto a load of hay Joseph Martin had just driven up.

Darius: But he is still going to be the Preacher some day?

Jacob: Vogel cannot say his esses very well now.

Darius: Can he not?

Jacob: When he landed on the hay he bit the tip off his tongue.

Darius: It is quite probable that Vogel will become the Preacher.

Jacob: The bosses said he was vain of his faith. They said he was setting it above his love of God.

Darius: Still ... the Lord did save him. And Joseph Martin. Oh ... and the load of hay.

Jacob: I am going to be a good boy. I am not going to ever blow music out of a little mouth organ.

Darius: *(Rising.)* Wanting to make music with a little mouth organ ... that is not sinful. Come over to the counter with me, Jacob. *(They go over to the counter.)* See them. *(Wong appears.)* They are very splendid. There is one taken out of its scarlet box and placed upon the lid.

Jacob, in spite of himself, has bent over and is peering at them intently.

Wong: *(Lifts mouth organ from counter.)* Buyee mouth ohgan ...buyee foh make music ... not listen my juice box on othah peopoh nickoh.

Jacob: Oh no ... please.

Darius: Jacob, I am going to give you something.

Jacob: No ...

Darius: How much are they?

Wong: Lovely mouth ohgan. Dollah fi'ty cen'.

Darius: We'll take this one. *(Handing mouth organ to Jacob.)* Music is not wicked. I want you to have this, Jacob. I want you to learn to play it.

Jacob: I ... I must ... *(Takes it.)* Thank you ... *(Wildly.)* Peter, the Goose Boss, will be waiting ... I have kept him long after he will have his teeth. The dentist made his new teeth ... we came in today for his teeth!

Darius: Don't be afraid of the Goose Boss, Jacob.

Jacob: *(Moves to the door.)* I must go before he comes to look for me ... thank you for the little mouth organ.

Darius: Hide it away from the bosses. Play it when you are alone. Be a good boy and do it. If there is a devil in that ... If he is in it ... I can tell you this ... He's a little devil, Jacob ... Such a very unimportant little devil.

Jacob rushes out.

———◆———

Scene 2

Peter, the Goose Boss, is waiting. He sits hunched over and is a little sour and disconsolate. He works his mouth as he tries to acquaint his gums with his new teeth. He has a long and flowing white beard. Jacob appears and climbs up beside him.

PETER GERRIE. GLENBOW ARCHIVES.

Alberta Theatre Projects (1977):
Stanley Coles as Peter, the Goose Boss.

Peter: It was not right to keep me waiting, Jacob.

Jacob: I am sorry Uncle Peter. I thought you would be longer.
I thought you would still be in the beer parlour ... at
the dentist's.

*Peter jerks the reins of the buggy and it runs away. Jingle and creak of
harness. Pock-pock of horses hooves quickens. Town sounds fade away
during this scene and prairie road sounds take over.*

Peter: You be a good boy, Jacob. The Devil don't like good
boys, so you be a good boy Jacob.

Jacob: Yes, Uncle Peter.

Peter: The Devil is a lot like a weasel; in his thirty-six-inch thrashing machine he thrashes souls. He likes fat Hutterite souls ... mixes them with others to bring the grading up. He is a lot like a weasel.

Jacob: Your new teeth ... *(Tries for better look.)* They look nice.

Peter: His breath is hot. His eyes are red. He is pure evil.

Jacob: They shine very white. They are whiter even than your beard.

Peter: Are they? When he steps from his weasel hole, he leaves behind his footprints of drought scorching the prairie for miles ... They pinch a little.

Jacob: They are lovely and white like an egg. After you have peeled it. Your beard is so white ...

Peter: You be a good boy ... like Vogel Unger.

Jacob: Vogel says a beard could not be so white as yours unless there was some bluing[6] ... *(Meadow lark.)* He says it is not right to be so vain about a beard. He says ...

Peter: Let Vogel talk about beards[7] when he is old enough to be married and grow one himself ...

Jacob: ... just a little bluing in the wash water when you wash your beard ...

Peter: Do not listen to such talk! You are easily led in the ways of wickedness as it is! Darius was so too. Remember Darius when you are tempted.

---

[6]Used to whiten laundry.

[7]Hutterite men shave until they are married and then grow beards.

Jacob:	Yes, Uncle Peter.
Peter:	The soul of your brother Darius is doomed to damnation and everlasting hellfire. Remember that!
Jacob:	Yes, Uncle Peter. Do they still hurt?
Peter:	The top ones. At the back. It is like a saddle sore where they rub and rub.
Jacob:	Could you not take them out?
Peter:	I will keep eighty-nine dollars and fifty cents in my mouth where it is safe.
Jacob:	The Chicken Boss says he has not had any teeth for fifteen years.
Peter:	The Chicken Boss is jealous.
Jacob:	Just his bare gums, he said.
Peter:	It was the Chicken Boss himself who said to send your brother Darius away to ...
Jacob:	Yes, Uncle Peter.
Peter:	... the teachers' training school so we could have our own kind of teacher for our own kids. And how did he come back from the city? How ... what did Sodom and Gomorrah[8] do to him fifteen years ago? Your brother?
Jacob:	He smoked.

---

[8]Biblical cities of iniquity that God destroyed with "brimstone and fire" (Genesis 19:24-25). Sodom and Gomorrah have become synonymous with sexual sin in particular.

Peter: Yes ...

Jacob: He hanged pictures on the schoolhouse walls.

Peter: You did not see. You were not old enough to remember.

Jacob: But you have told me often enough, Uncle Peter.

Peter: You did not hear him teach the kids to sing songs. The Devil got his finger into our colony that time. The Devil won't get *your* soul, Jacob.

Jacob: No, Uncle Peter.

Peter: And there will be no more about bluing.

Jacob: No, Uncle Peter.

Peter: In the water for washing my beard.

Jacob: No, Uncle Peter.

Peter: Or about loving my white beard and my new teeth more than the Lord, My God?

Jacob: *(He is sneaking a look at mouth organ.)* No, Uncle Peter. *(Meadow lark.)*

Peter: The Devil is like a weasel ... very like. And the Devil is in women. He is pure evil, Jezebel![9]

Jacob::   Ah ... do they ... do they still hurt now, Uncle Peter?

---

[9]Has become a general name for a wicked or shameless woman. In the Bible she was Queen of ancient Israel (see I and II Kings for her story).

Peter: Yes ... they do. There is no reason for them to stop.

Music.

— · —

Scene 3

Susan: Such a good well—it was ...

Old woman: No Glauber salts[10] at all ...

Preacher: Faith we need—with our faith Mike will find water ...

Mike: No—no—not there ...

Bone-setter: Ninety-nine percent faith—one per cent Mike, the Pig Boss ...

Marta's mother: I hope he finds it—

Otto: So the kids got no excuse for not taking the bath anymore.

Mother: So there is water for the garden again ...

Vogel: Praith the Lord for the water thign he may thend through the willow wand ...

Bone-setter: The witching of water[11] is at best a superstition.

---

[10]Hydrate of sodium sulphate chrystals were discovered by Johann Glauber, a seventeenth-century apothecary, to have medicinal uses, and Glauber's salts became widely used as a mild laxative. Well water containing sodium sulphate would obviously not be a good thing.
[11]Water witching, or dowsing, or divining: using a forked stick to find underground veins of water.

KARIN TRAPPER IN THE DEVIL'S INSTRUMENT, SIMON AND PIERRE (TORONTO, 1972), C10.

Ontario Youtheatre at
Peterborough Theatre Guild (1972).

Mike: It moved—it moved there ... !

Otto: Superstition it is not ...

Mother: No—no!

Peter: What you using, Mike?

Mike: Willow.

Peter: Hazel's better ...

Mike: I got some movement already—see ...

Otto: Willow grows near water always—willow wand works better because it loves water ...

Peter: Willow's waterlogged—bellyful of water it's got—Hazel's thirsty for water ...

Mike: Hah-hah! That's it! Strong ...

Susan: Look at it—look at it!

Rachel: Pulling right down ...

Vogel: Mutht be loth of water thuckin' it down tho thtrong ...

Mother: Such a pull—a flowing well ...

Old woman: Flowing well ...

Vogel: Praith Hith Thweet Name for thending uth ... Praith Mike, the Pig Both.

Otto: Best water-witcher west of the Hairy Hills!

Peter: Pretty strong ...

Bone-setter: From down below the power pulls ...

Peter: For willow.

Bone-setter: ... down below and that is where the powers of darkness lie ...

Preacher: Stick to the backbone, Bone-setter! Spiritual to the Preacher belongs. God is everywhere—above—around us—below, and He has shown us here pure water in abundance once more. Take the wand from Mike—see for yourself ...

The Bone-setter steps back involuntarily. The Preacher holds out his hands to Mike, who turns the wand up and places it in the Preacher's hands but goes around the Preacher and with arms around his shoulders places the Preacher's hands on the arms of the wand with thumbs in the upright position. Mike's hands still cover the Preacher's as the wand quivers and then dives down. Not only does it dive, but it brings the Preacher with it to his knees.

Preacher: Praise God—Praise His Holy Name!

Cast: *(In reverent assent.)*
Praise the Lord ...
Blessed Jesus ...

KARIN TRAPPER IN *THE DEVIL'S INSTRUMENT*, SIMON AND PIERRE (TORONTO, 1972), C15.

Ontario Youtheatre at Peterborough Theatre Guild (1972).

Praise His Name ...
Amen—amen ...
Hallelujah ...
Mike, the Pig Boss, done it again ...

Preacher: Let us pray—

Some kneel, some stand, for prayer tableau. All hands put together for prayer—all have heads down except the Preacher, who looks aloft to where God is. Looking sideways, Vogel sees this, so as he usually does he squeezes his eyes tightly shut and raises his attention aloft like the Preacher's.

Preacher: Heavenly Father, we thank Thee for showing us where Your water lies—through Mike, the Pig Boss, and his willow divining-rod—for we have sorrowed that our old well was getting low and Thy children and Thy children's children's flocks and Thy children's crops were thirsting bad. Now they shall flourish again—especially if you can arrange for a half-inch of rain as well now that the wheat and the oats and the barley are in the shot blade stage.[12]

As he has prayed the sun has been setting and the sky is red and the faithful are silhouetted against the foothill and the prairie sky.

—————◆—————

Scene 4

Sleeping quarters. Jacob and Peter sleeping.

MUSIC: *Mouth organ up softly, softly.*

---

[12]The shot blade, or flag leaf, is the last leaf on grain stalk before the head of grain.

Jacob:	*(Dreaming. Voice over.)* I wonder—I wonder—why did he give me the little mouth organ—ice cream—pink— he was kind to give me the mouth organ and the ice cream. Why should he ask all those questions?
MUSIC:	*Into subtle Hell stuff.*
LIGHTS:	*Devil effect as Darius appears. Hell stuff.*
Darius:	*(Voice over.)* Your father—your mother—they live in the colony? Who looks after you, Jacob? How old are you, Jacob? I have one brother, Jacob. He is your age, Jacob. How do you know it's the Devil's music, Jacob? Does the Devil like beauty, Jacob? Who am I, Jacob— the Devil is pure evil, Jacob ...
MUSIC:	*Hell and turmoil.*

Jacob asleep and tossing.

Jacob:	*(Voice over.)* No—no—no he isn't—the Devil is like a weasel. He was not like a weasel—he gave me the mouth organ.
MUSIC:	*Softly the mouth organ takes up.*
Jacob:	I will make lovely music. I will blow all the songs. I will blow all I have ever listened to. I will play tunes that have never been played before. I will play them first. They will be beautiful tunes. Beautiful tunes. They will ...
MUSIC:	*Mouth organ up in Jacob's dream—music then into unlovely snoring note.*
Peter:	*(Tossing. Voice over.)* His breath is hot. Be a good boy Jacob. Don't be—Darius ...

LIGHTS: Dream effect fades to black.

MUSIC: *Up full with mouth organ, then into hymnal stuff.*

Scene 5

The colony. Morning.

A montage of scenes showing the colony awakening.

The patriarchs at the breakfast table—the Preacher in his intense head-back act of prayer; the other heads lowered along the table. Prayer finishes. As one they dive into their porridge.

Kitchen with Hutterite women busy at breakfast preparations, ladling oatmeal into bowls and handing them to the girls, who carry them into the dining hall. One woman is handing Marta the large steaming kettle from the stove. Marta walks towards the corridor door.

Scene 6

Men at the finish of their prayer ...

Preacher: Amen ...

Others: Amen ...

Mike: An' pray God—no more lumps in the porridge.

Peter: Mash with the back of the spoon.

Preacher: Lord helps those who help themselves.

Otto: ... mash their own porridge lumps out ...

Peter: ... with the back of the spoon. *(It was his wisecrack.)*

Women have been bringing on their stove, etc.

Marta's mother: Careful—careful with the lid—steam burn is
                   bad ...

Old woman: Steam is bad ...

Rachel has come on later ... braids flying ...

Susan: Here—here—your hair loose ...

She swings daughter over to the table end and begins on the one untidy braid ...

Susan: Shame—shame—sleep late and no time for the hair ...
                 Shame—shame ...

Old woman: Shame—shame ...

Susan: Just like the Devil your hair it did—make you look like
                 a young witch ... or worse—girls in the town and the
                 city ...

Women in the kitchen ... Marta's mother is the woman in charge of the breakfast preparations.

Mother: For lumps—no excuses—never.

Woman one: Never.

Mother: Always the same—lumps come—they from too fast adding the oatmeal ...

Woman one: Too fast adding ...

Mother: I told you that—stirring is important too, Ruth.

Ruth: I didn't stir it—Rachel ...

Rachel: You said you would—you said you would when I had to leave ...

Woman one: Never leave the porridge—it burned last week ...

Ruth: Not bad.

Mother: No—but the black taste was in it—Vogel Unger complained ...

Rachel: He always complains ...

Ruth: Without all his tongue he can't taste anyway ...

Other girls all laugh and possibly it is during this that Anna gets through to Marta. Marta's mother notices.

Mother: Marta—come—from her—away!

Laughter of the girls is quelled ...

Woman one: Oatmeal is so simple. Not like noodles.

Marta's mother simply hands Marta the kettle and Marta knows she is to take it out to the washstands for the men.

Mother: You have your turn on the bread today Ruth—this time—punch down hard ...

Woman one: Punch down hard.

Rachel: Pretend it's Vogel's face ...

All laugh ... Mother sends Marta off.

Mother: Marta—more wash water for the men maybe and make sure they didn't waste it.

<hr />

Scene 7

A rough washstand of two-by-fours, holding a wash basin over which Jacob is bending. With one blind hand he is feeling for the long towel hanging on a nail in the wall.

Marta is standing there by Jacob holding the kettle. His reaching hand touches her kerchief—she steps back—he sees her for the first time.

Marta: Water. *(Breathless.)*

Jacob: Uh. *(Speechless.)*

Marta: Water—hot. *(Afterthought.)* Jacob. Here is a towel too. *(Holding one out.)* It is clean ... Jacob.

Jacob: Thank you.

Marta: It is a fresh one ... Jacob.

Jacob: I am all done.

Marta: Oh.

Jacob: Er ... except my neck ... I will need it for my neck.
              (Takes the fresh towel from her.) It is very dirty still ...
              it ... *(Clutching at the kettle which she holds.)* I will need
              hot water too.

Marta: Yes? *(Still holding the kettle.)*

Jacob: For ... for ... my neck ... my dirty neck.

Marta giggles.

*Jacob sees that they are both still holding the kettle handle. Marta
releases it. With his eyes still on her he absently pours it into the basin.*

Jacob: It gets dirty working the summer fallow.

Marta: Yes, Jacob.

Jacob: *(Unaware that as he still pours, the basin is flowing over
              its sides.)* Your eyes ... they ... they are ... they ...

Marta: Yes?

Jacob: Blue. Very blue ... I should not ... it wasn't right for
              me ... I ... I ...

Marta: No? *(Giggles again.)*

Jacob: Yes, looking at them. It was looking at them ... Marta ...
              that ... that ...

*He drops the emptied kettle with a clang. He turns from her and plunges
his face into the basin and begins furiously to wash his face.*

Marta laughs. She picks up her kettle and walks towards the kitchen door.

＊

Scene 8

Kitchen with women. Marta enters, still laughing.

Marta's mother looks back over her shoulder from the stove where she is stirring something or other.

Mother: Marta ... here ...

Marta: More water, Mother ...

Mother: Where have you been ... what have you ... you *got* water, girl!

Marta: It spilled ...

Mother: You be a good girl, Marta. *(Taking kettle from Marta.)* You were not talking to Walter or Anna?[13]

Marta: No, Mother.

Mother: What is wrong with you?

Marta: Nothing is wrong, Mother. He spilled the water ...

Mother: Who spilled the water?

---

[13]Walter and Anna are being "shunned" or "shamed" by the community, a process which is designed to encourage them to repent for their transgression so that they can be forgiven by God and rejoin the community.

Marta: Jacob.

Mother: Jacob Schunk! Now you be a good girl, Marta. You look
               at poor Anna and you be a good girl.

Marta nods in acquiescence.

Mother: That was how it started with Anna ... giggling and
               laughing with Walter. And look how it ended with
               Anna ... look ... straw stacks and three months of no
               talking. Don't you talk with her, Marta! It will be isola-
               tion for you too! Do not go near her or Jacob Schunk!
               You hear?

Marta, with head down, nods obediently.

⟫•⟪

Scene 9

MUSIC: *Mouth organ's rather crude efforts at hymn tune.*

Straw stack. Jacob seated with knees up and wide ... elbows resting upon them as he leans against straw stack in evening light.

He finishes the last bars of the hymn tune, and lowers the mouth organ slowly.

Jacob: Ahhh ... there is music from the little mouth organ
               and it was not so hard. It was not so hard at all ... just
               the hymn tunes ... that cannot be sinful to play hymn
               tunes only ... that is not the Devil's music. It cannot be
               wrong to feel this way ... this strange *(Lifting elbows
               and mouth organ.)* feeling that is so daring and so fine
               and ...

Jacob begins the rolling chords of hymn-like music. Orchestra takes it up in a sort of mouth-organ concerto. Carried away by his music, Jacob rises.

MUSIC: *Hymn music breaks and slips into bouncing, bawdy, earthy "Red River Valley," picked out by mouth organ. Orchestra breaks off to leave mouth organ alone carrying the tune. Mouth organ breaks off.*

Jacob: No! No! That is the Devil's music.

———◆———

Scene 10

Women spinning.

Rachel: Spinning I don't mind; carding[14] I hate. Grease all over the fingers.

Ruth: Dirt.

Rachel: It is all for the good of the colony.

Susan: Rachel is right, our young girls can learn a lesson from Rachel.

Ruth: Like snooping into people's hope chests.[15]

Susan: Kleinsaucer, the Sheep Boss, says the shed is full and another shearing is ready.

---

[14]Using a toothed instrument to untangle wool fibres before spinning.
[15]Box in which young unmarried women collect various items in anticipation of marriage—obviously Rachel has peeked in Ruth's hope chest.

Ruth:	*(Whispering to Rachel.)* Kleinsaucer, the Sheep Boss, does not look like a sheep—he looks like a she-goat.
Mother:	Girls, girls we must keep ourselves free from worldly things.
Rachel:	You mustn't say things like that.
Mother:	Not listening again, girls?
Ruth:	Yes—oh yes ... *(Parroting.)* We are free of worldly things ...
Mother:	But it was something else Ruth said to you ...
Rachel:	*(Female version of righteous Vogel.)* She said ...
Ruth:	Rachel!
Rachel:	What she said ... she said the Sheep Boss ...
Ruth:	Tattle-tale!
Rachel:	The Sheep Boss does not look like a sheep. *(She turns and smiles sweetly at Ruth, who is utterly relieved that Rachel has not squealed on her.)* Instead—*(Very quickly as she stabs her dearest friend.)* he looks like a goat!

All laugh ...

Old woman: Girls—girls! That is disrespect!

Ruth: Very like—very like ...

Old woman: Ruth!

Ruth: With his little red chin beard that wags when he talks and when he talks—*(She cannot suppress a giggle.)* he bleats ...

Mother: Girls—girls—Ruth—no more—not nice it isn't ...

Girls' laughter subsides and just as it has died down ...

Ruth: Baaaaaaaaa!

All burst into a gale of giggling—but then as they look over to Anna they turn it off like a cold-water tap.

Mother: *(To Marta)* Away from Anna Kleinsaucer.

———◆◆———

Scene 11

Spinning building. Women are chatting—working cleaning wool. Spinning.

Mother: Marta! More wool, girl! Marta ...

Marta: Yes. I am going—now ... *(She moves off.)*

Mother: Go straight to the shed—no fooling on the way—and on the way back, Marta. Straight there and straight back now! Just remember Anna and Walter if you think about stopping maybe. Jacob Schunk is no better than Walter Staebler—it was not long ago that maybe Anna was giggling just with Walter, and look at her now. *(Pause.)* Straight there—straight back, Marta.

Scene 12

Wool shed. Jacob waiting. Colony yard.

Marta, crossing yard, sees Jacob and responds—surprised—a little frightened ...

Marta: Oh! It is you—Jacob.

Jacob: Yes—I was—just—Uncle Peter—On my way—the— the geese ...

Marta: *(Pointing back beyond Jacob.)* But they are the other way—beyond the horse barns.

Jacob: Oh. Are they? Are they. Yes—I should—they are.

Mother: *(From kitchen.)* Marta—the wool! Girl ... the wool ... we are waiting!

Marta: Yes! In a moment. Jacob.

Mother: Marta!

Marta: In a moment. Jacob—you must not do this—we will be seen and it is not right!

Jacob: Seen!

Marta: No one speaks now to Anna or Walter!

Jacob: I know—but ...

Marta: Two weeks of isolation, already! She is in there now and no one dares speak to her.

Jacob: It is bad for Walter too ...

Marta: No one dares look at her even, for it will mean as bad for them.

Jacob: Today at lunch, Vogel was laughing and he saw Walter's face and he stopped right in the middle, and ...

Behind Jacob stands the Oats and Barley Boss.

Marta: *(In terrified warning.)* Jacob! Jacob!

Oats and Barley Boss: What is this! What is this! Jacob Schunk—You are not with Peter, the Goose Boss ...

Jacob: I—he has sent me—I came to—I was going to ...

Oats and Barley Boss: Marta Schreiber—you are not with the women.

Marta: I came outside to ...

Oats and Barley Boss: I can see that.

Marta: *(In a rush.)* And I saw Jacob pass—and I was to tell him to bring wool from the sheep.

Oats and Barley Boss: Profit by the sight of Anna, the Preacher's daughter, and Walter, son of the Wine Boss. See them as they move through days that are hushed and lonely. See conversation cease at their approach. See laughter and all eyes turned from them. For they have been now gifted with the power to blight. The shadow of their straw-stack sinning does travel always before them. The wrath of the Lord has descended down upon them. His angered hand lies upon their smothered hearts— Now—about your work—both of you *(Meaningful pause.)* No—straw stacks!

———◆◆◆———

Scene 13

Dining hall. Evening worship.

Preacher: Always we must watch—we must be ready, for he is waiting to get into our colony. Till now he has not got into our colony but he has new ways—last year he tried to ride into our colony on a self-propelled combine— and he did ride into the other colony on the four tractors they bought. These are machines of the Devil![16] *(Various degrees of assent from the other bosses.)* He will sneak into the colony through the radio and he will sneak into the colony any way he can. But we must watch—and we must guard. It is the Devil speaking through the Massey-Harris agent trying to sell us machinery, and what does his machinery do? All it does is take work away from the men and from the boys so they have all kinds of time to hide a radio in

---

[16]The Preacher and his colony are very traditional in their attitude towards farm machinery. But up to the 1940s there was great disagreement among colonies as to whether or not farm machinery was a temptation from the Devil. Many Hutterite colonies became even more progressive in their farming methods and machinery than their non-Hutterite neighbours. In an article for *Maclean's*, Mitchell commented on the colonies' changing attitude towards technology: "a more progressive colony bought a truck and a member from a more conservative colony warned: 'You can drive to hell in a truck.' And the retort was 'Lots of people drive to hell with a team and wagon.' And the answer came back: 'Maybe—yes—but you get to hell faster in a truck.' Today all colonies have the most modern in industrial equipment." "The People Who Don't Want Equality," *Maclean's*, July 3, 1965, 37.

the straw stack and listen to the Devil's music out of there. All it does is give them time to think of other things they should not think about. These are machines of the Devil. Mostly, the Devil tries to sneak in through the young ones—the ones that have the flesh to itch—the unmarried ones—like Anna and Walter now in isolation. The Devil does not like married men *(The other patriarchs agree to this.)*—so we must watch—watch for the boys and girls that are looking at each other—watch for the ones that blush and the ones that laugh too much—watch for them and remember them and watch them more carefully. *(Pause.)* These are the ones that the Devil is making to blush and to laugh—these are the ones that will marry in the fall—before harvest.

Scene 14

Straw stack. Jacob with knees up at his straw stack in evening light. He stares down at the mouth organ held in his hand ...he lifts it to his mouth, then takes it away ... he stares at it with distaste—then rises to his feet with sudden determination ... he crouches and scoops a hole in the straw stack. Begins to bury it there—hesitates—then buries it and turns away—seats himself—stares out disconsolately—then back and takes mouth organ out and puts it to his mouth ...

MUSIC: *As in previous scene—hymnal at first ... his foot keeping time to the music.*

The music slips and slides into quite unreligious stuff ... Jacob's eyes are closed. He is lost in the bouncing ecstasy of his cowboy ballad.

Breaks suddenly.

Jacob: No! No! *(He falls to his knees. Hands up. His eyes tightly shut.)* Our Father: the stranger gave me the little mouth organ and I have used it. I blew through it and played music. Forgive me and I will not do it again— ever—I will not blow through the wooden teeth to make songs. I will not even blow the hymns, O Lord, let alone "The Strawberry Roan"[17] and "The Death of Pete Knight"[18] and—"Going to Go to Heaven on a Streamline Train."[19] I will not. I promise. Amen—Lord.

Lights fade out.

———◆———

Scene 15

Lights fade up.

Jacob and Peter sit against the straw stack set ... daytime.

SOUND: *Meadow lark a couple of times, the gabble of geese from flocks off—background.*

Peter: Jacob. Jacob.

Jacob: Yes, Uncle Peter.

Peter: *(Bending forward and pretending great interest in Jacob's chin.)* What is that on your face?

---

[17]A cowboy ballad originally written by Curly Fletcher in 1915; it became a popular country-western song in the 1920s and 1930s.
[18]Pete Knight was a famous bronc rider who started his riding career in Alberta during World War I and won four World Bronc Riding Championships. He was killed in a rodeo bronc competition in California in 1937.
[19]"I'm Gonna go to Heaven on a Streamline Train," a cowboy song sung by a very popular Canadian country music singer Wilf Carter (also known as Montana Slim).

Jacob: *(Alarm.)* On my face!

Peter: *(Smiling.)* In no time at all you will be growing a beard. By fall, perhaps. Marriage and a beard—they go together, Jacob.

Jacob: Marriage! A beard!

Peter: In fall ... there will be marrying. The Devil don't like married men so good. Marta.

Jacob: We have not been ...

Peter: There was a meeting of the bosses last night. The bosses are not blind, Jacob.

Jacob: But we had not ...

Peter: Marta is a good girl. You could have lots of kids. In fall, Jacob. If you wish—if Marta wishes ...

Jacob: I do—I do—she—oh—Uncle Peter.

Scene 16

The yard. Back end of wagon box—on a trip to town they would use an ordinary wagon box and team—piling in as many as possible ... perhaps a visit to the town dentist—perhaps to the liquor vendor's with permits to get the month's supply of liquor—for the most part there is no feeling about liquor, though there is about tea, coffee, tobacco.

We see Hutterites of all ages and sizes piling out of the wagon—the last one comes over the end seat first ...

Vogel-Unger stands looking about, then as he sees Jacob in the distance...

Vogel: Jacob—Jacob—there wath a man! Do you know he wanted to thee you! He athked to thee you in town, Jacob!

Jacob: Man—wanted ...

Vogel: He ith not one of the people from the town. He had jutht come, he thaid. Do you know—he ith thtaying at the hotel. Do you know he wanth to thee you?

Jacob: But why—who is he? What did he say his name ...

Vogel: He jutht came where we were doing the machinery. "Do you know Jacob Schunk," he thaid—"Do you know whether he ith coming into town? Do you ... "

Jacob: Was he tall? Did he look like John the Blacksmith?

Vogel: He had no beard—of courth, he hadn't any at all ...

Jacob: I know—but with a beard—then would he look like John the Blacksmith? Did he?

Vogel: I couldn't tell.

Jacob: Are you going in tomorrow? Are—could you let me go in your place, Vogel?

Vogel: We are going all thith week, but I could not—you couldn't.

Jacob: Just tomorrow—that will be enough. Tell them—ah— you could have a—tell them you do not feel well tomorrow.

KARIN TRAPPER IN *THE DEVIL'S INSTRUMENT*, SIMON AND PIERRE (TORONTO, 1972), C24.

Ontario Youtheatre at Peterborough Theatre Guild (1972).

Vogel: But—it dothn't—they—that would be lying!

Jacob: Vogel—you do not feel well at all—your head aches—
your back hurts.

Vogel: But—it dothn't—it doth not! They don't—at all.

Jacob: They will tomorrow! You will have to go the Bone-
setter and tell him ...

Vogel: Oh, no I won't! Do you know—I never felt better?

Jacob's ominous face.

Jacob: If you do feel well tomorrow, Vogel—do you know,
Vogel—then you are going to have to go the
Bone-setter anyway!

Scene 17

Palm Café. Darius at the counter, buying a package of cigarettes.

Darius: Small, please—cork tips.

Wong: *(Reaching down for cigarettes.)* Oh yeah—oh yeah—thirty-foh cen'—make thirty-fi' you take match. *(Tosses Darius packet of matches.)* Why bothah peopoh penny—why thirty-foh, why not thirty-five cen'. Make law—no penny law so peopoh don't fool with penny all time.

Darius: I guess so.

Wong: Everythin'—fohty-nine—fifty-nine—thirty-foh—dollah seventeen—nasty penny—*(Picks up Chinese paper he's been reading behind counter—mutters into paper.)* No more penny law! Utterly no more penny—law against pennies all ovah Canada!

Darius moves back to a booth. There he sits, looking up anxiously from time to time.

Jacob: *(Enters.)* I am looking for somebody ...

Wong: Oh sure—sure—no kind you peopoh here today—

Darius rises.

Darius: Jacob. Jacob—Jacob Schunk!

Jacob: *(Pause.)* Hello.

Darius: Well, how are you, Jacob?

Jacob: *(Going towards him.)* I played the little mouth organ.

Darius: That's nice, Jacob. *(Darius sits down.)*

Jacob: *(Sitting down with him.)* You told Vogel Unger you wanted to see me.

Darius: Yes. Yes, Jacob. *(He does not know quite how to get on with it.)* You see, ah—I have a special interest—I am *(Weakening.)* I was once—I once belonged to our—your people. I was twenty when I left the colony—twenty years, Jacob, is a long time to eat the bread of security—to have all your decisions made for you by the bosses. Perhaps I have not lost—all that—that weakness. *(Pause.)* Outside the city—just outside—where I live—there is a colony ...

Jacob: There isn't any colony near the city ...

Darius: Not the same kind, Jacob. In this one they have different prisoners. Each morning they take the men out in the trucks to work the beet fields. Each night they take them back to sleep inside. It is called a jail, Jacob. When I have passed the camp, I have thought of you, Jacob. Each time. There are guards there with guns instead of bearded bosses. The fence is higher. But those are slight differences. They—are—so—slight.

Jacob: Who are you?

Darius: My name is Darius. I—I—am your brother, Jacob. I am Darius.

Jacob: You say it like that. You are my brother.

Darius: Yes. I have dreamed of coming for you and taking you away with me, but when you told me who you were that day I could not do it.

Jacob: Could you not?

Darius: I wanted to, but I couldn't. When I returned to the city I cursed myself for not bringing you back with me.

Jacob: That was all right—Darius. I guess it was all right—Darius.

Darius: Because you are not free either, Jacob—it—you are not free in body or in soul. None of you are—not even the Oats and Barley Boss.

Jacob: Oh no—it is not like that ...

Darius: None of you are! The colony is not God's way! It is wicked!

Jacob: Not wicked, Darius!

Darius: Freedom is light, Jacob! The way of the Lord is a shining light—the way of the wicked lies in the shadow and darkness of ignorance and bondage!

Jacob: Our people are not wicked!

Darius: There are three things. There is truth, and that is the best thing. There are freedom and beauty too, and the Devil hates all these things. Truth and beauty are the same—and that's all you need to know, Jacob. A poet[20]

---

[20]Darius is quoting from John Keats's "Ode on a Grecian Urn," which speculates on the profound impact the ideal world of art has on the real world of human affairs.

said that, and he is not one of our—your people. Our people have no poets ... for the colony kills what is beautiful ... it will not let beauty grow ... it cannot grow without freedom!

Jacob: But—I have found ...

Darius: *(Overriding him with all stops out.)* The Devil wears hook-and-eye fasteners right down his ugly homespun jacket! He has a long beard and he is Boss over all the Bosses!

Jacob: No—No—that is not true!

Darius: *(The fire fades slowly from his face, then quite gently.)* I am sorry, Jacob.

Jacob: You say there is no beauty in the colony. *(Pause.)* There is Marta.

Darius: Marta?

Jacob: John the Blacksmith's daughter.

Darius: Oh.

Jacob: The first time—here—you asked me if I was happy in the colony. Well—I am happy ... now.

Darius: I see.

Jacob: I do not—not play the little mouth organ—*(Pause.)* now.

Darius: Did it make you unhappy, Jacob?

Jacob: Are you happy outside the colony, Darius?

Darius: Happy? *I am free!*

Jacob: Are you happy, Darius?

Darius: Happiness is not everything. I must be honest with
                you. I am free. Anyway—I am free.

Jacob: *(Blurting it.)* I am going to be married. *(Pause.)* I am
                going to marry Marta.

Darius: Are you? Are you, Jacob?

Jacob: Soon.

Darius: That is their hold—that is the bosses' strongest hold.
                They make that work for them, too.

Jacob: You do not understand, Darius. Last night I walked
                with Marta from the pump to the kitchen. We did not
                talk. We came to a patch of mud. We both stepped
                aside—in the wrong direction. She touched me,
                Darius. I felt her hand against the back of mine. It
                was lovely—it was aching lovely.[21] I could not
                breathe, Darius.

Darius: You will never leave. *(Pause.)* After you are married. I
                am married now. I met her soon after I left the colony
                to go to the teachers' school. Women are important,
                Jacob. They are not weak. One takes me from the
                colony. Another holds you to it.

---

[21]Another Keats echo: see "aching pleasure" in "Ode on Melancholy."

Jacob: *(Slowly and gently—his voice almost breaking.)* I am
sorry—Darius. *(He gets up and walks away from the
table.)*

*Darius gets up as though to go after him and bring him back, then sinks
back into his seat. Wong comes to the booth. He looks down at Darius a
moment—the other man staring at his hands before him on the table.*

Wong: He go. *(Pause.)* No ice cream. *(Pause.)* Mouth ohgan.
(Long pause. Darius looks up.) I remember—long time
here—I remember—you buy too befoh—you don't
buy mouth ohgan then. Don't smoke cigarettes then
too. *(Pause.)* You smoke cigarette now. *(Long pause. He
shrugs.)* Same thing China—all kinds peopoh—come
along—all kinds peopoh do different—after while
change—

━━━◆◆◆━━━

Scene 18

Straw stack. Evening.

*Jacob burying mouth organ—when he has finished he stays on his knees
and looks up to wherever the Hutterite God hangs out.*

Jacob: *(Half to himself, half to God.)* Like I promised—I keep
it. No more music out of the mouth organ—not
anymore. It is a trade and I will marry Marta and not
play the mouth organ. I buried away the mouth organ
for Marta Schreiber, daughter of John the Blacksmith,
because she is more beautiful than any music out of a
mouth organ and it is a good trade. I have traded with
You for good—the mouth organ for the soft brush of
her hand—for the curve of her cheek. And I would
please want another thing. My brother is a good man,

Ontario Youtheatre at Peterborough Theatre Guild (1972):
Miles McNamara as Jacob.

he is not wicked. Do not turn your face from him—
save him from doom and eternal damnation. *(Pause.)*
And—and—*(He looks back to where the mouth organ is
buried.)* give me a little help—to let it stay buried—
perhaps I can see Marta once before we are married—
just once alone ...

Scene 19

*Kitchen. Women, Marta—Anna sits alone from the others as they
prepare the supper meal. Marta carries a pail of potatoes over to Anna,
seated—she stoops low as she sets down the pail.*

Marta: *(Whispering.)* Hello, Anna—it will end, Anna—they will not be silent to you forever … *(She looks up.)*

Mother: Marta! Here—

Marta straightens up, leaves Anna … heads for door.

Anna alone and tragic—begins to peel the potatoes, if that can be a tragic act.

Outside in the yard, Jacob standing—obviously waiting. Marta appears in door.

Jacob: Marta—Marta—Please may I see you—alone?

Marta: Oh, no—Jacob—we must not! We …

Jacob: Tonight—the straw stack! Please!

Marta: It is only a month now, Jacob!

Jacob: Please, Marta! You must—you must!

Marta: The Preacher—the Sheep Boss—they are coming—we will be seen!

Jacob: I will be there, Marta! I will be there!

Marta is wildly shoving Jacob away.

Marta: No—no—go now—I won't—you shouldn't—it is not fair. Yes, Jacob—Dear God—yes!

Jacob, joyful, exits. Marta watches him leave—she turns and goes across the yard on her errand.

Scene 20

Anna: *(Whispers fiercely.)* Marta, oh—oh, Marta ... *(Marta does not leave her but she doesn't answer her.)* You were my closest friend, Marta ...

Marta: Sh-sh, Anna—don't ...

Anna: Just touch me, Marta—my hand ...

With glances toward the older women, Marta does—hiding the friendly touch from the older women ...

Anna: I—it is so terrible, Marta—I am alone in the whole world—or else in the world—I'm not any more—at all ...[22]

Marta: All right—all right, Anna—you aren't—I think of you—so I keep you alive in myself ...

Anna: I can't stand it any more!

Marta: It will end—they will not be silent from you for ever ...

John the Blacksmith: Marta!

Marta is startled since she has not seen her father come up.

John: Be a good girl, Marta. *(A gesture of his hand sends her off—he turns and stares down at Anna, who has turned*

---

[22]Anna feels as if she no longer exists, as if her community has "vanished" her. This is a theme Mitchell explores more fully in *The Vanishing Point* (see the scene in which Carlyle feels that he has been "vanished" by Old Kacky, 309–314).

KARIN TRAPPER IN *THE DEVIL'S INSTRUMENT*, SIMON AND PIERRE (TORONTO, 1972), C28.

Ontario Youtheatre at Peterborough Theatre Guild (1972).

her head down to the potatoes. She is crying now—John the Blacksmith places his hand on her shoulder.) Little Anna—be a good girl too—your punishment is almost over—the silence will lift from you soon.

The Preacher comes over to them. John turns to him.

John: I've told her—just now.

Preacher: You were not told to tell her.

John: Someone told me to tell her ...

Preacher: I didn't tell you to ...

John: No, not you—somebody from the meeting—I was
alone and His Voice came to me in the wind that
travelled in a funnel over the summer fallow—and His
Voice told me to tell her—and the wind was gentle and
warm—

Preacher: You have disobeyed ...

John: I obeyed His Voice that was in the wind. I obeyed Him
when He told me to tell Anna—I think you must listen
to that wind better, Preacher—when it blows through
our colony. It is the wind of compassion.

*The Preacher has no answer to this. John takes his hand from Anna's
shoulder and turns away from her and the Preacher.*

—————

Scene 21

*Just outside the kitchen where the old well is, Mike and Otto are taking
out the pump to go to the new well.*

Mike: Just new leathers[23] and she will be working like new—
good deep well, double-piston pump ...

Otto: Sure—over twenty years we didn't have to prime
much ...

Mike: Almost as old as the colony here—don't drop it, that
little brass plug ... work better in the new well, even ...

---

[23]Leather seals (cup-leathers) are used inside the cylinder of hand pumps to draw the water
up the main pipe when the handle pumps the piston.

just like us—works good—he must have been
Hutterite, eh?

Otto: Who?

Mike: Mr. Wisconsin[24]—Hutterite made good religion back
there with Martin Luther—Menno Simmons—Jacob
Hutter[25] ... Mr. Wisconsin made good piston pump,
too.

*John and Preacher have come out of the kitchen and are carrying on
their exchange from when they were in with Anna ...*

John: They are spirit but they are flesh too ...

Mike: But I guess Moses made the first one when he hit the
rock with his staff, eh?

John: ... and they must grow to beauty and goodness ...

Preacher: Not to wickedness—the world will seduce them into
it—we must shield our children from the ways of the
world—they must fear God.

---

[24]Mike is confused here. The pump is not named after its inventor, but after the state in
which it was manufactured (Wisconsin, United States).

[25]Martin Luther launched the Protestant Reformation against the Catholic Church when, in
1517, he nailed his criticism of the Church to the door of Wittenburg Cathedral. Among
other things, he argued for the primacy of the Bible and faith unmediated by Church
authority. In the previous scene, John is acting as a latter-day Martin Luther when he bucks
the Preacher's authority by acting on his own intuition and faith and criticizes the Preacher
for his lack of compassion. Menno Simmons was ordained as a Catholic priest; he rejected
Catholicism in 1536 and became an Anabaptist religious leader. He was the founder of the
Mennonites. Jacob Hutter (Jacob's namesake) was an Anabaptist religious leader during the
Reformation who founded the Hutterites. The Anabaptists believed in adult baptism
which, during the Reformation, was a criminal offense and punishable by death. For his
beliefs, Hutter was tortured and burned alive in 1536.

John: ... *Love* God.

Preacher: Do not rely on love too much! Without fear—there is danger! We have done for Anna Kleinsaucer a great thing to save her soul from eternal damnation—we will do it for others—I warn you, John the Blacksmith—the father can be blind to the signs that are clear to others—sin signs in his own flesh and blood. They are not easy to see always!

Mike: Preacher's right ... sometimes I think it's too bad we didn't have some kind of wand—like my willow for divining the water—a wand we could hold in our hands and pass it over them and tell us where the sin welled strong. *(Brings himself up as he realizes this is ridiculous.)* But of course what kind of wood—could do that?

Preacher: That which the Lord used, Pig Boss—in the garden of Eden—apple tree!

Scene 22

Jacob: Marta—oh, Marta ...

Marta: Jacob! It is wrong! You shouldn't ...

Jacob: I wouldn't ask you to do wrong, Marta! I don't want us to do wrong at all!

Marta: We have done it now ...

Jacob: I have—you haven't. I will not any more—because of you! You are everything now. I told God—

Marta: You shouldn't ask me to ...

Jacob: I had to see you—

Marta: I'm afraid, Jacob! I don't want to be like Anna—I don't want to die from everyone like Anna ...

Jacob: You won't—you won't—I promise you won't ...

Marta: Maybe Walter said that to Anna.

Jacob: It's all right, Marta!

Marta: Not for Anna ...

Jacob: No one will know ...

Marta: What did you tell God?

Jacob: I told Him—I told—I told Him I love you more—I told Him I loved you more than the little mouth organ—*(Catching himself up.)* Not more than Him—but Marta—it is a lot I love you! I had to tell you that, Marta! I had to! Is that wicked to tell you that—just to tell you that!

Marta: *(Pause.)* I don't think it is.

Jacob: Oh, Marta!

Marta: Jacob—I love you a lot too.

Jacob: Marta, Marta ...

Clinch.

Scene 23

Straw stack. Morning.

Morning sounds: geese.

Lights fade up—to discover Jacob lost in reverie.

Peter: *(In his own reverie.)* The Devil don't like married men. *(Long pause.)* You want to marry Marta. *(This is a statement of fact.)* You want to grow a beard—have kids. Be a good boy, Jacob. *(Long pause.)* You were not. *(Shaking his head sadly.)* You were not—*(Pause.)* last night.

Jacob is startled from his reverie.

Peter: I do not sleep so well, Jacob. *(Pause.)* You left.

Jacob: *(Seems about to protest, then lowers his head in admission.)* Yes, Uncle Peter.

Peter is sadly shaking his head.

Peter: Straw stacks.

Jacob: Yes—no! I tell you it is not like that. *(Springs wildly to his feet.)* I did see Marta last night—but it's not what you think—we—we just stood ...

Peter: Yes, Jacob?

Jacob: I—we could feel the night air cooling against our cheeks—it was—the smell of hay and the wild mint— it was beautiful, Uncle Peter.

Peter: Was it, Jacob?

Jacob: It would make the spit come to your mouth.

Peter stares with understanding at Jacob—gently nods his head ... reaches up to take Jacob by the arm and gently pull him down beside him ...

Peter: I had my straw stack too, Jacob. When I was young ... before I could grow a beard, the Devil came to me in the city one day. He found me on the street with a bag of money in my hand. It was colony money. The Devil told me to buy a new suit for myself. *(Wistful—ah, wistful this whole confession of youthful folly many, many years ago.)* The pants had creases in them. It was a sort of green suit. Pretty. I wore it that day. Right out of the store. I met a woman with red hair. She wore a blue dress like a violet. She lived with a lot of other Jezebels on the edge of the city and she called me her little geranium flower. I was going to take her away from that place, but in the Chinaman's café she unscrewed the top from the stool and hit the waiter over the head. *(Still the incredibly gentle and sweet reverie.)* She screamed very loud—long—she swore wicked too—she threw their spittoon through the whole window. Twenty dollars for the green suit with creases in the pants. Ten dollars for the wine. Five dollars for the Jezebel. Fifteen dollars for the window. Thirty dollars for the Chinaman. Fourteen dollars for the judge. *(Long and contemplative pause.)* Sin comes expensive, Jacob. A sinful life could run a man as high as two hundred dollars a month. *(He turns his head to look at Jacob and see how this astronomical figure strikes him.)* There are worse things, Jacob, than being lonely in the colony. You could be lonely outside the colony too. Like your brother—Darius.

Jacob: I know, Uncle Peter.

Peter: Be a good boy, Jacob! *(This is a fierce plea.)*

Jacob: I will, Uncle Peter! *(This is just as fierce a promise.)*

SOUND: *Meadow lark's four notes above the background gabble of goose ... as light fades.*

Scene 24

Straw stack. Night. Night sounds. Jacob arrives at the straw stack—drops to his knees.

Jacob: I do not see her—I am not meeting her any more by the pump—I do not even look into her eyes when she serves at the table. I will wait till we are married. I have been good two weeks—but—*(He falters.)*

Jacob's hand on the straw—it feels around—goes into the straw—comes out with the mouth organ—he looks down at it.

SOUND: *Coyote howls distantly, and train whoops on the night silence ...*

Jacob lifts the mouth organ—puts it hesitantly to his mouth—makes it do the long interrogative whoooooooo-whoooooooo of the train. He lowers it and sighs as with relief. He gives in and begins to play, hymn-like, sad ...

Jacob stops playing—lowers his elbows—knocks the organ against the side of his palm to shake the condensed saliva from its space teeth. His elbows rise up and out again. Closes his eyes. Plays again.

MUSIC: *Orchestra now with mouth organ riding high and lyric.*

Jacob lets mouth organ buck, his feet tap. His body sways ecstatically with the music.

Peter comes on. He grabs Jacob—wrenches the mouth organ from his hands.

Peter: I told you! I warned you, Jacob! I told you to be a good boy!

CBC Television, Folio (1956): Jack Creley as Peter the Goose Boss; Douglas Rain as Jacob.

Scene 25

Oats and Barley Boss: *(Clears throat portentously.)* Jacob Schunk—you have sinned. *(There is the deep assent of male voices.)* Peter, the Goose Boss, say before us what you know and let him deny it.

Peter: *(Rising to his feet by the Judgment Table.)* I wakened in the middle of the night. I had to go outside. I am not a young man anymore. I heard a sound. It came from the south forty straw stack. I went there. *(He turns and throws out an accusing arm.)* I found him! He had that in his hands. *(He points to mouth organ.)* I called to him. He did not hear me. He was blowing into it, so music came out of it.

There are clicking sounds of disapproval from the bosses. The Preacher hawks in his throat—sounds die down to utter silence.

SOUND: *Rooster off—crows loud and clear and long—the sound stretching like an elastic band.*

Oats and Barley Boss: Jacob Schunk, you have sinned. Let Peter say before us again what he knows; let Jacob deny it.

Peter: Four years ago, he set a trap line. He caught four weasels and a skunk. He turned in to the Hide Boss three weasel pelts and a skunk. He took the weasel pelt hidden in his jacket to the hide buyer in town. He got fifty cents for it. He bought a bag of Maple Bud candies. He also bought five ice cream cones from Wong, the Chinaman at the Palm Café. He ate three and he gave one to Vogel Unger and another to Otto, the Sheep Boss's son. Behind the livery stable.

The members of the court make their deep male herd sounds again. The Bone-setter belches accusingly.

Oats and Barley Boss: Jacob Schunk, you have sinned. Let Peter say further what he knows. Let Jacob *deny* it.

SOUND: *The second clear call of the outside rooster.*[26] *Peter's head is thrown back. He has been working himself up into an evangelistic fervour. For the first time since his fall from grace with the Calgary hooker of his youth, he is now one of the orthodox fold. It is a fine and wonderful feeling and the moment of his greatest triumph.*

Peter: He sneaked out in the middle of the night. He met Marta, the daughter of John the Blacksmith. It was at the straw stack in the south forty. He kissed her on the mouth. She kissed him back. I saw them do this. I saw them.

The court murmuring again.

Oats and Barley Boss: Jacob Schunk, pay attention. We are not angry with you. We want you to know that. We wish only to turn you back from the path of wickedness. To save your soul from eternal damnation. Your punishment is this. You shall be apart. No one shall come near you. Everyone shall turn his eyes from you. No one shall speak to you—for three months. To do any of these things shall be as great a sin as those you have committed. *(Many of the court nodding slow approval of the sentence.)* You shall not blow through the mouth organ again. John the Blacksmith shall place it on his

---

[26]Peter's betrayal of Jacob and the crowing rooster echo the disciple Peter's betrayal of Christ in the Bible (see Matt. 26:74–75).

KARIN TRAPPER IN THE DEVIL'S INSTRUMENT, SIMON AND PIERRE (TORONTO, 1972), C31.

Ontario Youtheatre at
Peterborough Theatre Guild (1972).

anvil and he shall smash it. Marta, daughter of John
the Blacksmith, shall have one month's isolation. When
the fall marrying comes, she shall not marry you, Jacob
Schunk. We will not lose a soul—another—soul.

Jacob: *(As this part of the sentence sinks in)* Marta! It is not fair
to punish Marta ...

Oats and Barley Boss: *(Rising.)* We will sing now a hymn.

Jacob: She had nothing to do with the mouth ... *(Oats and
Barley Boss begins first line of old chanting German
hymn.)* ... organ. She—the weasel pelt ... (Two deeper

voices join the voice of the Oats and Barley Boss.)—It is
not fair that ... *(Louder to make himself heard)* ... it is
not fair that ... *(More voices in the relentless hymn)* ...
she should be punished too ... *(All voices now in the
chanting hymn—Jacob is fairly screaming to make
himself heard.)* Listen—listen to me! I will not stay—if
you do this to Marta, I will—damn your black fat
souls—I will—GO—OOOOOO! *(He is lost now, in the
full strength of the men's singing.)*

Scene 26

The kitchen.

Mother: Don't touch the lid after the dough is dropped ...

Susan: It makes the dumplings sad ...

Old woman: Makes them sad ...

Susan: Nothing's worse than sad dumplings ...

Old woman: Nothing's worse ...

Ruth looks over to the lonely Marta.

Ruth: Yes, there is nothing worse than sad dumplings ...

Rachel: Sin is worst—wicked, wicked—straw-stack sin ...

Anna: Stop it—stop it ...

Rachel: You ought to know, Anna ...

Ruth: Leave her alone ...

Rachel: Yes—that's just what we are to do ...

Woman one: Girls—girls—

Scene 27

The kitchen. A bustle of activity—but over by herself, Marta sits with hands in her lap, apart from the others. A woman pauses by her ... she looks up to speak, then realizes she must not—woman passes her—her mother comes and hands her a pail silently, indicates the door with a silent nod of her head. Marta gets up slowly with the pail—moves to the door ...

Jacob is waiting outside for her ...

Jacob: Marta—Marta! *(Stricken and frightened, she turns away and runs past him—Jacob runs after her.)* Please— Marta! *(She struggles to be free from him.)* Marta—I am leaving—I want—Marta, come with me—my brother, Darius—(He seizes her by the shoulders—she struggles.) Marta—Marta—please Marta—please—just listen. *(She breaks away and runs back towards the kitchen.)*— You don't have to talk—All I want you to do is listen! *(He reaches her half-way to the kitchen door and grabs at her again.)* There is nothing wrong with listening, is there! You don't have to say anything ... *(She breaks from him again and runs to the kitchen door and inside.)* Marta—I am going away ... *(He brings up against the slammed door.)* Please, Marta—(He beats against the closed door.) Marta—listen—(Beating again.) You will listen to me! All of you—listen to me! I am going!

Leaving! All of you—this is your chance to hear! Can your ears hear this—damn you all! Oh damn you, all of you—I leave you all!

⊸•◦•⊶

Scene 28

Palm Café. Wong and Trucker at counter—Trucker paying bill. Goes to jukebox—makes selection and inserts coin, then leans against counter to listen to the record play. Jacob enters—sees Trucker—goes to him. Trucker is turned slightly away and rapt in music. After a couple of false starts, Jacob plucks at his sleeve ...

Jacob: Please—*(Trucker turns and looks at him.)* Excuse me—

Trucker: Uh-huh?

Jacob: I—wondered—would—are you leaving?

Trucker: Huh?

Jacob: Are you going to drive away now? Right now? *(Trucker simply nods his head.)* To the—towards the city?

Trucker: Yep.

Jacob: *(After an awkward pause)* Would you let me ride?

Trucker: Uh-huh. *(Looks steadily at Jacob.)* No beard. No beard, so you ain't married. *(Laughs.)* No beard down your hook-an'-eye jacket, so you ain't ... *(Sees the boy is distressed.)* No offence, kid—sure—I can give you a lift. Sixteen—y'ain't old enough to get married yet—or grow a beard.

Jacob: *(Dully.)* I am old enough.

Trucker: What you goin' to the city for? Long ways—over a
                 hundred miles ...

Jacob: I have left the colony.

Trucker: *(Surprised.)* Oh—now—I wouldn't do that.
                 You—*(Grins.)* won't never grow a beard you
                 do that.

Jacob: No—I will never grow a beard now. Poor Marta ...

Trucker: Your girl?

Jacob: They punished her too—she would not—she could not
                 talk to me again—she was afraid.

Trucker: That why you're leavin'?

Jacob: Yes.

Trucker: Awful holt over you folks. Never heard of one of you to
                 cut loose before.

Jacob: My brother Darius did.

Trucker: Why'd he leave?

Jacob: He hanged pictures on the schoolhouse walls. He
                 smoked cigarettes.

Trucker: Catch you smokin'?

Jacob: No. I played some music out of a little mouth organ.

Trucker: That all! Just for blowin' a mouth organ! What you gonna do?

Jacob: If you give me a ride in your truck to the city, I am going to my brother. *(Pause.)* He wants me. *(Pause.)* He will buy me another mouth organ.

Trucker: Come on, then.

MUSIC: *Mouth organ alone in a simple happy air, possibly built on four-note meadow-lark song—orchestra takes it up for crashing and triumphant finale. Jacob Schunk may not know it, but this is victory ...*

Alberta Theatre Projects Program (1977). Puppets designed by Pat Flood.

PRODUCTION HISTORIES

—◆—

THE BLACK BONSPIEL OF WULLIE MacCRIMMON

Radio

1950:   Half-hour radio play, CBC *Summer Theatre*, July 30. Produced by Peter MacDonald. Music by Lloyd Edwards.

1951:   One-hour radio play, CBC *Stage 51*, February 25. Directed by Andrew Allen. Music by Lucio Agostini. Frank Peddie as Wullie MacCrimmon; Alan King as O. Cloutie; William Needles as Reverend Pringle; Alan Pearce as Pipe-fitting; Alex McKee as Cross-cut; Tommy Tweed as Malleable; John Drainie as Don Fletcher; Bud Knapp as the Narrator.

1954:   One-hour radio play, CBC *Stage 54*, February 28. Director and cast as for Stage 51 production.

1955:   One-hour radio play, CBC *Folio*, October 9. Frank Peddie as Willie MacCrimmon; Lloyd Bochner as O. Cloutie.

1968:   One-hour radio play, CBC *Stage*, March 3. Produced by E.W. Ljungh. Music by Morris Surdin.

Television

1955:   One-hour television drama, CBC *Folio*, October 9. Directed by Robert Allen. Music by Louis Applebaum. Frank Peddie as Wullie MacCrimmon. This was Mitchell's first television drama.

1962:   One-hour television drama, CBC *Playdate*, March 7. Directed by Melwyn Breen. Produced by Robert Allen. John Drainie as Wullie MacCrimmon; Ed McNamara as O. Cloutie; with John Horton, Hugh Webster, Drew Thompson, Larry Beattie, Paul Kligman, Gertrude Bradley, Jay Shannon, Donald Ewer, and Tony Parr.

Stage

There have been over seventy productions of *The Black Bonspiel* staged by professional, amateur, and school groups. The following, apart from the Lakefield College School production, is a selected list of most professional productions.

1966:   Staged by The Grove Players of Lakefield College School. Andrew Harris, English master, adapted the television script (published in *Three Worlds of Drama*), for stage as a one-act play. His production won the awards for best overall play (competing against adult amateur, university, and high school groups), best high school play, best director, and best actor at the 1966 Eastern Ontario One-Act Drama Festival.

1977:   Staged by the Peterborough Festival of Canadian Theatre with two other plays, July 15 to August 27. Directed by Guy Sprung. Hugh Webster as Wullie MacCrimmon; Geoffrey Saville-Read as O. Cloutie; and Maja Ardal as Annie Brown. W.O. adapted the play, moving it from the prairies to Peterborough in Depression times.

1979:   Staged by Theatre Calgary at the QR Centre, March 6 to 31. Directed by Guy Sprung. Set design by Pat Flood. Sound design by Michael Becker. Hugh Webster as Wullie MacCrimmon; Michael Ball as O. Cloutie; Stephen Hair as Reverend Pringle; Sharon Bakker as Annie Brown; David Francis as Pipe-fitting; Jean-Robert Greenwood as Clock; Pierre Fournier as Malleable; James Eberle as Guy Fawkes; Paul Jolicoeur as Judas Iscariot; and Jack Ackroyd as Macbeth.

1980:   Remount of 1979 production, with some cast changes. Staged by Theatre Calgary, March 4 to April 5. Directed by Guy Sprung. Set design by Pat Flood. Hugh Webster as Wullie MacCrimmon; Paul Jolicoeur as O. Cloutie; Stephen Hair as Reverend Pringle; Sharon Bakker as Annie Brown; David Francis as Pipe-fitting; Ray Landry as Clock; Robert Koons as Malleable; James Eberle as Guy Fawkes; Steven Schipper as Judas Iscariot; and Jack Ackroyd as Macbeth.

1980: Theatre Calgary production, under the auspices of the Festival of Arts, toured Alberta June 10 to July 4 in celebration of Alberta's 75th anniversary. Hugh Webster was replaced by Leslie Carlson as Wullie MacCrimmon. It played at the Citadel Theatre in Edmonton, June 30 to July 4, then toured eight Alberta centres, from Lethbridge to Peace River.

1980: Staged at the Lennoxville Festival in July. Directed by Rick McNair. Hugh Webster as Wullie MacCrimmon.

1982: Staged by the Manitoba Theatre Centre, December 31, 1981 to January 23, 1982. Directed by Rick McNair. Set and costumes by Arthur Penson. Lighting by Robert Thomson. Wayne Robson as Wullie MacCrimmon; Robert Benson as O. Cloutie; John Innes as Reverend Pringle; Nancy Drake as Annie Brown; Andrew Gillies as Pipe-fitting; Richard Vincent-Hurst as Clock; Owen Foran as Malleable; Robert MacDonald as Guy Fawkes; Peter Smith as Judas Iscariot; and Brian Paul as Macbeth.

1982: Staged by the Vancouver Playhouse, September 22 to October 23. Directed by Walter Learning. Design by Michael Nemirsky. Lighting by Donald B. Scarrow. Sound and original music by William Skolnik. Eric House as Wullie MacCrimmon; Ted Follows as O. Cloutie; Ross Douglas as Reverend Pringle; Daphne Goldrick as Annie Brown; Guy Bannerman as Pipe-fitting; Peter Elliot as Clock; Jack Ammon as Malleable; Mark Wilson as Guy Fawkes; Christopher Trace as Judas Iscariot; and Colin Miller as Macbeth.

1982: Staged by the Citadel Theatre, October 26 to November 21. Directed by Frances Hyland. Set and costumes by Bill Layton. Lighting by Allan Stichbury. Music and sound by Michael Becker. Hugh Webster as Wullie MacCrimmon; Claude Bede as O. Cloutie; Brian Taylor as Reverend Pringle; Miriam Newhouse as Annie Brown; Al Kozlik as Pipe-fitting; Frank C. Turner as Clock; Wally McSween as Malleable; Richard Gishler as Murphy; Allan Lysell as Nero; and Peter Messaline as Macbeth.

1983:   Produced by the Western Canada Theatre Company at the Sagebrush Theatre, Kamloops, January 13 to 22. Directed by Michael Dobbin. Set design by Donald Halton. Lighting by Sharon Wade. Keith Dinicol as Wullie MacCrimmon; Jack Northmore as O. Cloutie; Bill Dow as Reverend Pringle; Mary Ann Coles as Annie Brown; Wes Tritter as Pipe-fitting; Allen MacInnis as Clock; Michael Bianchin as Malleable; Michael Dyson as Guy Fawkes; James Leyden as Judas Iscariot; and Rod Christensen as Macbeth.

1983:   Staged for the Kawartha Summer Theatre, Lindsay, July 12 to 16. Directed by David Gardiner. Set design by Christopher Adeney. Dan MacDonald as Wullie MacCrimmon; Dennis Simpson as O. Cloutie; Ray Doucette as Reverend Pringle; Alex Stockwell as Pipe-fitting; Don Blakeley as Clock; Daniel Legault as Guy Fawkes; Joshua Major as Judas Iscariot; and Bruce Latimer as Macbeth.

1985:   Staged by Theatre Aquarius, Hamilton, April 24 to May 18. Directed by Peter Mandia. Set and costume design by Jonathan Porter. David Glyn-Jones as Wullie MacCrimmon; John Bayliss as O. Cloutie; Jean Daigle as Reverend Pringle; Helen Bell as Annie Brown; Roger Dunn as Pipe-fitting; David Mallis as Clock; Bill McDermott as Malleable; Dee R. McCafferty as Guy Fawkes; Allen Stewart-Coates as Judas Iscariot; and Gerald Lenton as Macbeth.

1985:   Staged by Theatre Newfoundland and Labrador, February 7 to 9. Directed by Edmund MacLean. Production design by Ian Mennie. Jerry Etienne as Wullie MacCrimmon; Robert Dodds as O. Cloutie; John Dancey as Reverend Pringle; Julia Rank as Annie Brown; Bob Richards as Pipe-fitting; Bob Butt as Clock; Tommy Murphy as Malleable; Gary Kelly as Guy Fawkes; Rae Smith as Judas Iscariot; and Brian Smith as Macbeth.

1986:   Staged by Neptune Theatre, April 25 to May 18. Directed by Glen Cairns. Set and costume design by Robert Doyle. Lighting by David Ingraham. Don Harron as Wullie MacCrimmon; Maxim Mazumdar as O. Cloutie; Glenn

White as Reverend Pringle; Catherine McKinnon as Annie Brown; Bill Carr as Pipe-fitting; Kelly Handerek as Clock; Joseph Rutten as Malleable; Scott Owen as Guy Fawkes; Martin Millerchip as Judas Iscariot; and Shawn Wright as Macbeth.

1986:   Staged by Huron County Playhouse, July 15 to 26. Directed by Steven Schipper. Set design by Brian Perchaluk. Lighting by Grant T. Smith. Costumes by Yvonne Sauriol. Lewis Gordon as Wullie MacCrimmon; David Clark as O. Cloutie; James Haworth as Reverend Pringle; Aileen Taylor-Smith as Annie Brown; David Francis as Pipe-fitting; Stan Coles as Clock; G. Peter Henderson as Malleable; Alan Brown as Guy Fawkes; Murray Oliver as Judas Iscariot; Paul Massel as Macbeth; and Mark Mollard and Mellissa Brock as Town Children.

1986:   Staged by the Sudbury Theatre Centre, January 15 to February 2. Directed by Bob Clout. Set design by Bob Ivey. Lighting by Simon Day. Costumes by Warna Timlock. Donald Saunders as Wullie MacCrimmon; John Bayliss as O. Cloutie; Donnie Bowes as Reverend Pringle; Suzanne Cotton as Annie Brown; Paul-Emile Frappier as Pipe-fitting; Ron Tough as Malleable; Steve Spera as Guy Fawkes; Marvin Ishmael as Judas Iscariot; and Ron Payne as Macbeth.

1987:   Staged by Theatre New Brunswick, April 10 to May 4. Travelled throughout New Brunswick, opening in Moncton, with seven performances in Fredericton and thirteen in eight other locations. Directed by Michel Lefebvre. Set and costumes by Pat Flood. Lighting by Louise Guinand. Music by Cathy Nosaty. Mo Beck as Wullie MacCrimmon; Mark Wilson as O. Cloutie; Lorna Wilson as Annie Brown; David Mallis as Pipe-fitting; Vaughn Fulford as Clock; Philip Williams as Malleable; David McKnight as Guy Fawkes; Simon Bradbury as Judas Iscariot; and Doug Hughes as Macbeth.

1988:   Staged by Theatre Calgary, November 25 to December 17. Directed by Douglas Riske. Set design by Nigel Scott.

Costume design by Pamela Lampkin. Lighting by Christopher Hall. Brian Tree as Wullie MacCrimmon; William Webster as O. Cloutie; Stephen Hair as Reverend Pringle; Heather Lea MacCallum as Annie Brown; Frank C. Turner as Pipe-fitting; Jim Leyden as Clock; Jean-Pierre Fournier as Malleable; Brian Gromoff as Guy Fawkes; Howard Siegel as Judas Iscariot; Wally McSween as Macbeth; Howard Siegel as Announcer; and Brian Gromoff, Jim Leyden, and William Webster as Townspeople.

1990:   Staged by The Globe Theatre, Regina, October 12 to 20. Directed by Kim Selody. Set design by Helen Jarvis. Costumes by Michelle Latta. Lighting by Ralph A. Skanes. Music by Rob Bryanton. Jim Timmins as Wullie MacCrimmon; Bill Rowat as O. Cloutie; Dwight McFee as Pipe-fitting; Tom Rooney as Clock; Wayne Nicklas as Malleable; Darrell Baran as Reverend Pringle; Richard Hughes as Judas Iscariot; Julien Arnold as Guy Fawkes; Gerry Mackay as Macbeth; Megan McArton as Annie Brown.

1991:   Staged by Richmond Gateway Theatre, Richmond BC, October 17–26. Directed by John Cooper; set design by Ross Nichol; Costumes by Pearl Bellesen; lighting by Jennifer Bergron. Bill Dow as Wullie MacCrimmon; Alex Diakun as O. Cloutie; Andrew Wheeler as Reverend Pringle; Dwight McFee as Pipe-fitting; Wes Tritter as Clock; March Acheson as Malleable; Doug Abrahams as Macbeth; Laurier Dubeau as Guy Fawkes; Eric Epstein as Judas Iscariot; Crystal Verge as Annie Brown.

1993:   Staged by Theatre Aquarius, Hamilton, October 27 to November 13. Directed by Peter Mandia. Set and costume design by Maxine Graham. Lighting by Paul Mathiesen. Sound by Darrell MacLean. David Glyn-Jones as Wullie MacCrimmon; Stephen Russell as O. Cloutie; Andrew Dolha as Reverend Pringle; Helen Beavis as Annie Brown; Roger Dunn as Pipe-fitting; David Mallis as Clock; Richard Binsley as Malleable; Marc Richard as Guy Fawkes; Dean

Hollin/Adrian Parkinson as Judas Iscariot; and Victor Ertmanis as Macbeth.

1994: Staged by Blyth Festival, August 3 to September 3. Directed by Ted Johns. Set design by Pat Flood. Gordon Milroy as Wullie MacCrimmon; Dennis Fitzgerald as O. Cloutie; Robert Persichini as Reverend Pringle; Anne Anglin as Annie Brown; Cliff Saunders as Pipe-fitting; Jerry Franken as Clock; Thomas Hauff as Malleable; Andrew Croft as Guy Fawkes; Thomas Albrecht as Judas Iscariot; and David Young as Macbeth.

1995: Staged by Prime Stock Theatre Company, Red Deer, February 29 to March 17. Directed by and set design by Thomas Usher. Costume design by Selena Percy. Lighting design by Trampas Brown. Sound design by Gina Puntil. Andrew Hamilton as Wullie MacCrimmon; Brett Manyluk as O. Cloutie; Rory Crockford as Reverend Pringle; Annette Scheper as Annie Brown; Murray Utas as Pipe-fitting; Kevin Corey as Clock; Brent Jans as Malleable; Michael Kuss as Guy Fawkes; Michael Cherrington as Judas Iscariot; and Serge Bellieveau as Macbeth.

1996: Staged by Western Canada Theatre Company at the Sagebrush Theatre, Kamloops, February 22 to March 2, as part of the 1996 Kamloops Labatt Brier. Directed by Kevin McKendrick. Set design by Michael Cade. Costume design by Janis Cliffe. Lighting by Linda Babins. Sound by Doug Perry. Keith Dinicol as Wullie MacCrimmon; James Fagan Tait as O. Cloutie; Barry Thorson as Reverend Pringle; Danielle Dunn-Morris as Annie Brown; Bruce Parkhouse as Pipe-fitting; Larry Lefebvre as Clock; Grant Linneberg as Malleable; Henry Small as Judas Iscariot; Brian Jensen as Macbeth; Sheda Petersen as Lizzie Borden; and Marlene Hauk as Angel.

1997: Staged by Alberta Theatre Projects and Mount Royal College at the Martha Cohen Theatre, Calgary, March 7 to 16. Invited by the Calgary Brier Society to perform during the 1997 Labatt Brier. Directed by Michael Dobbin. Set design by Scott Reid. Costume design by Madeline Brian. Lighting by Brian Pincott. Gerald Matthews as Wullie MacCrimmon; Doug McLeod as O. Cloutie; Stephen MacDonald as Reverend Pringle; Clarice Evans as Annie Brown; David Barrett as Pipe-fitting; David Shelley as Clock; Chad Nobert as Malleable; John Shearer as Judas Iscariot; Steve McIntosh as Macbeth; and Kella Glen as Lizzie Borden. This was a community production using Mount Royal College production people who were mentored by ATP professionals, and starring a combination of professional and local talent.

1999:   Staged by Thousand Island Playhouse, Gananoque, May 12 to June 13. Directed by Mo Beck. Gordon McCall as Wullie MacCrimmon; Mathew Gibson as O. Cloutie; J.D. Smith as Reverend Pringle; Karen Skidmore as Annie Brown; Bill Fisher as Pipe-fitting; Scott Hurst as Malleable; Mark Hunt as Guy Fawkes; Gord Muir as Judas Iscariot; and Mark Ingram as Macbeth.

2004:   Staged in French, *Le Bonspiel sinistre de Wullie MacCrimmon* (translated by Laurier Gareau), by La Troupe du Jour in Montreal, October 14 to 17. Directed by Ian C. Nelson. Set design and lighting by David Granger. Costumes by Denis Rouleau. Julien Thibeault as Wullie MacCrimmon; Adrienne Sawchuk as O. Cloutie; Raoul Granger as Le Révérend Pringle; Réjeanne Brière as Annie Leblanc; Bruno Bourdache as Jean-Cadran Leblanc; Richard Kerbes as Jean-Tuyau Leblanc; Jean-Marie Michaud as Jean-Malléable Leblanc; Brigitte Chassé as Guy Fawkes; Laurence Royez-Guérin as Judas Iscariote; and Colette Jako as Macbeth.

2004:   Staged by Grand Theatre, London, February 3 to 21. Directed by Michael Dobbin. Set design and costumes by John Dinning. William Vickers as Wullie MacCrimmon; Robert Benson as O. Cloutie; David Snelgrove as Reverend Pringle; Douglas E. Hughes as Pipe-fitting; David Kirby as Clock; Thom Marriot as Malleable; Eric Trask as Judas Iscariot; Kurtis Sanheim as Macbeth; and Rachel Holden-Jones as Lizzie Borden.

Print

1945:   First written as a short story; unpublished.

1964:   Short story published in an abridged prose version in *The Curler*. December, 1.6.

1966:   Television script published in *Three Worlds of Drama*, ed. by Jack Livesley. Toronto: Macmillan of Canada. Other plays were Tennessee Williams's *The Glass Menagerie* and Herman Wouk's *The Caine Mutiny Court-Martial*.

1976:   Novella published by Frontier Publishing, Calgary.

1980:   Stage play version published in *Canadian Theatre Review*. Spring, 26: 58–107.

1982:   Stage play version published in *Dramatic W.O. Mitchell*. Toronto: Macmillan of Canada. 101–141.

1993:   Novella version: *The Black Bonspiel of Willie MacCrimmon*. Toronto: Douglas Gibson/McClelland & Stewart. With 10 illustrations by Wesley W. Bates.

THE DEVIL'S INSTRUMENT

Radio

1949:   One-hour drama, CBC *Stage 49*, March 27. Produced and directed by Andrew Allan. Music by Lucio Agostini. William Needles as Jacob Schunk; Lloyd Bochner as Darius; Budd Knapp as the Devil;[1] Toby Robbins as Marta; John Drainie as Peter, the Goose Boss; Henry Karpus as Vogel Unger; Mavor

---

[1]In this first radio adaptation of his novella, Mitchell created an additional character, the Devil, who plays a substantial role throughout the story (in the novella, the Devil is only implicit in Darius who tempts Jacob with the mouth organ). In the first of the Devil's thirty-five speeches, he says, "I'm a travelling man. I travel in sin. I travel in souls (PAUSE) wholesale souls and retail sin" (MsC 19.20.1, Mitchell fonds, University of Calgary), lines which Mitchell later used for the Devil character in *The Black Bonspiel of Wullie MacCrimmon*.

Moore as the Oats and Barley Boss; Jerry Sarracini as Jake; Alan King as Wong; and Tommy Tweed as Trucker.

1953:   One-hour drama, CBC *Stage 53*, November 8. Produced and directed by Andrew Allan. William Needles as Jacob Schunk.

1959:   One-hour drama, CBC *Stage*, April 26. Produced and directed by James Kent. Also aired on BBC, United Kingdom on June 4.

Television

1956:   One-hour drama, CBC *Folio*, November 21. Directed by David Greene. Douglas Rain as Jacob Schunk. The CBC *Folio* series won first place at Ohio University, Columbus, annual television awards, and *The Devil's Instrument* won special mention for "inspired television writing" (*CBC Times*). W.O. wrote to his mother about this production: "That young man Douglas Rain was terrific as Jacob and David Green is a most imaginative director. My only difference with them would have been that they did not allow a little more of the laughter and gaiety of the colony show through. Marta was directed to a little too solemn an interpretation so that the mood was somewhat unrelieved and somber. Otherwise it was terrific." On March 11, 1957, the Canadian Council of Authors and Artists presented *The Devil's Instrument* with the award "for most distinguished artistic and creative achievement in English radio, TV, and cinema" for 1956.

1958:   Kinescope of above production shown at Brussels World's Fair on August 10.

1959:   Shown on television throughout the United Kingdom on June 13.

1962:   One-hour drama, CBC *Festival*, November 5. Directed by Eric Till. Douglas Rain as Jacob Schunk; Ron Hartman as Darius; Ingi Bergman as Marta; John Drainie as Peter, the Goose Boss; Peter Mews as the Preacher; Alice Hill as Marta's Mother; Robert Christie as the Oats and Barley Boss; Alexander Webster as Jake; George Chow as Wong.

Stage

1972: Staged by Ontario Youtheatre at the Peterborough Theatre Guild, August 10. Ron Hartman directed the production and trained a company of thirty-two actors, designers, and technicians. Miles McNamara as Jacob Schunk; James Love as Darius; Pippa Smyth as Marta; John Norris as Peter, the Goose Boss; Harry Warr as the Preacher. W.O. Mitchell worked with Hartman in Peterborough on this production, augmenting the television script with material from the radio version. The play was taken to eight major cities in Ontario, including Brockville, London, and Ottawa for a total of sixteen performances.

1977: Staged by Alberta Theatre Projects at the Canmore Opera House, Heritage Park, Calgary, September 26 to October 21. Directed by Douglas Riske. Set design by Pat Flood. This production used actors for the six core roles and life-size puppets for the secondary roles, which were manipulated by the six actors. Brian Paul as Jacob Schunk; Faye Cohen as Marta; Teresa Tova Krygier as Marta's Mother; Stanley Coles as Peter, the Goose Boss; Gordon Stokoe as Darius; Robert Clinton as One Other Man. This production was seen by 1600 Junior High School Students in Calgary. A booklet of "Teachers' Preparatory and Follow-up Material" was prepared in conjunction.

1982: A dramatic reading, arranged by Canadian Cultural Programmes, in the auditorium of the Royal Bank Building, Place Ville Marie, Montreal, June 7.

1985: Reading by W.O. Mitchell, with improvised harmonica, percussion, and piano, Music Inter Alia Inc., Winnipeg, February.

Print

1949: Novella submitted to Atlantic/Little Brown and to Macmillan. Macmillan agreed to publish in Fall 1949 with illustrations by William Winter, but advance notice of an American novel, *The Dream Gate* by Marcus Bach, resulted in the cancellation of publication by Macmillan since it was remarkably similar in subject matter.

1972: Published in *A Collection of Canadian Plays*, Vol. I. ed. by Rolf Kalman. Toronto: Simon and Pierre. C: 1-31.

1982: Published in *Dramatic W.O. Mitchell*. Toronto: Macmillan of Canada. 2-38.

1987: Stage 49 production script published in *All the Bright Company: Radio Drama Produced by Andrew Allan*. ed. by Howard Fink and John Jackson. Kingston: Quarry Press, CBC Enterprises. 30-66.

BIOGRAPHICAL CHRONOLOGY

1914: William Ormond Mitchell, second of four sons, was born to Ormond (a pharmacist) and Margaret (McMurray) Mitchell on March 13 in Weyburn, Saskatchewan.

1921: Death of Ormond, his father, on April 5, which indelibly marked him and was the genesis for *Who Has Seen the Wind*. Grandfather McMurray died on August 30 and Grandmother Maggie McMurray, also an inspiration for *Who Has Seen the Wind*, moved into the Mitchell household.

1926: Contracted bovine tuberculosis in the fall and was withdrawn from school. This contributed to his becoming a writer, for he frequently wandered the prairie alone, developing a keen sense of observation of the natural world and becoming reflective, particularly about mortality.

1927: Moved to California for the winter months to cure his tuberculosis.

1928: From 1928 to 1931 attended high school at St. Petersburg, Florida. Through his English teacher he developed a strong interest in drama and took the lead role in the High School production of *Skidding*.

1931: From 1931 to 1934 attended University of Manitoba, first enrolled in the sciences, then transferred to the arts when his tuberculosis flared up and he had to abandon the study of medicine.

1934: From 1934 to 1935 worked and studied in Seattle, Washington. He enrolled at the university in a class on journalism, short story writing, and drama, where he wrote three one-act plays.

1935: Returned to Canada in the fall and for five years took on odd jobs: selling advertisement space, insurance, encyclopaedias, and magazines; teaching diving; and even doing a high-dive act at a summer carnival.

1940:   Moved to Edmonton where he completed his B.A. and received his Teacher's Certificate from the University of Alberta. He met Merna Hirtle who introduced him to F.M. Salter, English and creative writing professor at the university, who encouraged the writing of the Jake and the Kid stories and *Who Has Seen the Wind*.

1942:   Married Merna Hirtle and moved to Castor, Alberta, where he taught and was principal of the high school. Here he was introduced to curling. "But as Yesterday" published in *Queen's Quarterly*. "You Gotta Teeter" and " Elbow Room" published in *Maclean's*.

1943:   Spent the summer in Edmonton where Orm, their first child, was born. In the fall, became principal of the New Dayton high school. Here he met the Hutterites for the first time and witnessed the scene in the café of the young Hutterite boy's desire to own a harmonica that became the genesis for his novella and drama *The Devil's Instrument*.

1944:   Lived in Weyburn and in Edmonton where he worked on *Who Has Seen the Wind*.

1945:   Moved to High River, Alberta.

1946:   Second son, Hugh, born.

1947:   Publication of *Who Has Seen the Wind* by Atlantic Monthly Press and Macmillan Canada. Began writing his second novel, "The Alien." Worked on the short story *The Black Bonspiel of Wullie MacCrimmon*.

1948:   Lived in Toronto from 1948 to 1951, where he was fiction editor at *Maclean's*.

1949:   *The Devil's Instrument*, his first one-hour radio drama, adapted from his novella for CBC *Stage 49*, March 27.

1950:   From 1950 to 1956 wrote over 200 stories for the hit CBC radio drama series, *Jake and the Kid*. *The Black Bonspiel* adapted for radio as a half-hour drama on Summer Stage, July 30.

1951:   *The Black Bonspiel* expanded to a one-hour drama, broadcast on CBC Stage 51, February 25. Returned to High River in April. From fall 1951 to April 1952 he taught at Eden Valley, the Stoney Indian Reservation.

1952: Taught his first writing workshop at Qu'Appelle and returned there each summer until 1956. Returned to Eden Valley to write "The Alien" from fall to February 1953.

1953: "The Alien" finished but rejected by Little, Brown. It won the first *Maclean's* new novel award and Part III was published in the magazine. Adapted "The Day Jake Made Her Rain" into a one-act play which was produced by the summer drama workshop at Qu'Appelle.

1954: Third child, Willa, born. Decided against publishing "The Alien" with Macmillan.

1955: His first television drama, *The Black Bonspiel of Wullie MacCrimmon*, produced by CBC *Folio*, October 9.

1956: *The Devil's Instrument* produced by CBC *Folio*, November 21. He began writing "Roses Are Difficult Here." In the fall, he began adapting his Jake and the Kid stories for a joint television series with CBC and NFB.

1959: *Royalty is Royalty*, a three-act play, produced by Greystone Players, Saskatoon.

1960: His mother died September 20. He began writing reminiscential pieces about his childhood years.

1961: Published short story collection, *Jake and the Kid*, for which he won the 1962 Leacock Medal for Humour. Decided not to publish "Roses" with Macmillan. CBC ran twelve television dramas of *Jake and the Kid* from July 4 to September 19. *Foothill Fables*, a series of radio dramas, ran December 25 to January 19, 1964. Anti-Hutterite sentiment on rise in High River area to prevent them buying more land. Mitchell wrote "No Man Is," a radio drama for CBC's *Summer Fallow*, May 29, to show the positive value of Hutterite society.

1962: Published novel *The Kite*.

1963: Suffered from depression for two years. Wrote television documentaries.

1964: *The Kite*, a one-hour radio drama, produced by CBC Summer Stage, June 12.

1965:   First of his one-man performances at MAC Theatre, Calgary, February 20. From this point onward he was in constant demand for readings, lectures, key-note addresses, and radio and television interviews. At the peak of his performance career in the mid-1980s, he would often be doing eight to ten performances a month. *The Kite*, a one-hour television drama, produced by CBC *Show of the Week*.

1966:   First stage production of *The Black Bonspiel* by Lakefield College School. Began writing novel *The Vanishing Point*.

1967:   *Wild Rose*, a musical drama, was produced by MAC Theatre, Calgary for a royal command performance before Princess Alexandra on May 24.

1968:   First writer-in-residence position at University of Calgary for three years.

1971:   Position at University of Alberta, teaching creative writing and literature.

1972:   Honorary degree received from University of Saskatchewan, Regina, the first of nine. Other honorary degress from Universities of Ottawa, Brandon, Alberta, Windsor, Calgary, Lethbridge, Trent, and Victoria.

1973:   .Published novel *The Vanishing Point*. Received the Order of Canada. Writer in residence at University of Toronto for one year.

1974:   Completed drama *Back to Beulah*, which was produced on CBC TV's *The Play's the Thing*, March 21 and on CBC radio, October 26, for which he won an ACTRA award for Best Writer. Wrote screenplay for *Alien Thunder* starring Donald Sutherland. Established the summer writing program at Banff, which he headed until 1986.

1976:   *Back to Beulah*, three-act stage drama, was produced by Theatre Calgary in January, Tarragon Theatre in Toronto in February, and Vancouver Playhouse in March. Wrote screenplay for *Who Has Seen the Wind* although it was not used. *Black Bonspiel* was staged by Stoneboat Theatre, Regina, February 1976. *The Day Jake Made Her Rain* was staged by Alberta Theatre Projects, January 26.

1977:   *Back to Beulah* won Chalmers Award for best play. Stage play, *Black Bonspiel*, produced by Peterborough Festival, July. Writer in residence at York University for one year. Completed first draft of film script for "Back to Beulah."

1978:   *Sacrament*, one hour CBC television drama, televised on January 1.

1979:   Writer in residence at University of Windsor for eight years. *Black Bonspiel* staged by Theatre Calgary in March and remounted next year due to its huge success.

1981:   Published novel *How I Spent My Summer Holidays. The Kite* staged by Theatre Calgary in April. *The Kite* staged by the Citadel Theatre in October, which won the 1981-82 Best Play Award. Premiere of *For Those in Peril on the Sea (Sacrament)*, Theatre 2000, Ottawa.

1982:   *Dramatic W.O. Mitchell*, collection of five plays, published. *For Those in Peril on the Sea* staged by Theatre Calgary, February.

1984:   Published novel *Since Daisy Creek.*

1988:   Published novel *Ladybug, Ladybug. The Black Bonspiel* staged by Theatre Calgary to capacity audiences. "W.O. Mitchell Day" declared in Calgary on November 28.

1989:   Published second collection of short stories, *According to Jake and the Kid*. Received the Lifetime Award for Excellence in the Arts from the Saskatchewan Arts Board Award.

1990:   Published novel *Roses Are Difficult Here*. Awarded the Leacock Medal for Humour for *According to Jake and the Kid*. Toronto International Festival of Authors paid tribute to Mitchell, October 18.

1992:   Named an honorary member of the Queen's Privy Council of Canada. Published novel *For Art's Sake.*

1993:   Published novella *The Black Bonspiel of Willie MacCrimmon.*

1994:   At work on his final novel, "Brotherhood True or False," which was never published.

1995:   Nelvana and Global Television began producing *Jake and the Kid* television series of thirteen episodes per year for two years.

1996:   Margaret Laurence Lecture for the Writers' Union delivered May 31, his final public performance.

1997:   Published collection of his reminiscential pieces and reading selections, *An Evening With W.O. Mitchell*.

1998:   Died in Calgary, February 25. Merna Mitchell died May 12.

BIBLIOGRAPHY

Alberta Theatre Projects Archives. Alberta Theatre Projects Office.

Brown, Stewart. "FX: When the Devil Himself Makes an Appearance on Stage, Theatre Aquarius Goes All Out for the Full (Special) Effects." *Hamilton Spectator*, November 9, 1993.

Citadel Theatre Archives. Provincial Archives of Alberta.

Dawson, Eric. "Behind the Scenes at the Black Bonspiel of Wullie MacCrimmon." *Calgary Herald*, March 1, 1980.

Grand Theatre Archives. Archival and Special Collections. University of Guelph.

Kucherawy, Dennis. "Devil Slides Out of the Hack to Win MacCrimmon's Soul." *Winnipeg Free Press*, December 30, 1981.

Hobson, Louis. "Mini-Mitchell Worth Encore." *The Albertan*, September 27, 1977.

Kirchoff, H.J. "Bonspiel a Good Match for Blyth." *Globe and Mail*, August 9, 1994. C.3.

Manitoba Theatre Centre Archives. Archives of Manitoba.

Milton, John. *Paradise Lost*.

Mitchell, Barbara and Ormond. *Mitchell: The Life of W.O. Mitchell. The Years of Fame, 1948–1998*. Toronto: McClelland & Stewart, 2005.

Mitchell, Barbara and Ormond. *W.O.: The Life of W.O. Mitchell, Beginnings to Who Has Seen the Wind 1914–1947*. Toronto: McClelland & Stewart, 1999.

Mitchell, W.O. *Dramatic W.O. Mitchell*. Toronto: Macmillan of Canada, 1982.

Mitchell, W.O. *How I Spent My Summer Holidays*. Toronto: McClelland & Stewart, 2000.

Mitchell, W.O. *Jake and the Kid*. Fredericton, NB: Goose Lane Editions, 2008.

Mitchell, W.O. "The People Who Don't Want Equality." *Maclean's*, July 3, 1965: 9.

Mitchell, W.O. *The Vanishing Point*. Toronto: Prospero Books, 2008.

Mitchell, W.O. *Who Has Seen the Wind*. Afterword by Barbara and Ormond Mitchell. Toronto: McClelland & Stewart, 2001.

Morrow, Martin. "The Devil and the Black Bonspiel." *Calgary Herald*, November 25, 1988.

Neptune Theatre Archives. Dalhousie University Archives.

"Pentecostals Seek Ban of Books from Schools." *The Albertan*, August 30, 1978.

Portman, Jamie. "Blyth Festival Back on Firm Footing." *Ottawa Citizen*. August 10, 1994.

Ryan, John. "Hutterites." *The 1999 Canadian Encyclopedia: World Edition*. CD-ROM. Toronto: McClelland & Stewart, 1998.

Sprung, Guy. "Acting W.O." *Magic Lies: The Art of W.O. Mitchell*. Edited by Sheila Latham and David Latham. Toronto: University of Toronto Press, 1997.

Theatre Aquarius Archives. Archival and Special Collections. University of Guelph.

W.O. Mitchell fonds. Special Collections. University of Calgary Library.

FURTHER READING

Benét, Stephen Vincent. *The Devil and Daniel Webster*. New York: Dramatist's Play Service, 2004.

Harrison, Dick. "W.O. Mitchell." *Canadian Authors and their Works*, Fiction Series. Vol. 4. Toronto: ECW Press, 1991.

Latham, Sheila and David Latham, Editors. *Magic Lies: The Art of W.O. Mitchell*. Toronto: University of Toronto Press, 1997.

Marlowe, Christopher. *Doctor Faustus*. Edited by Michael Keefer. Peterborough: Broadview Editions, 2007.

McNair, Rick. "W.O. Mitchell: The Playwright." *Magic Lies: The Art of W.O. Mitchell*. Edited by Sheila Latham and David Latham. Toronto: University of Toronto Press, 1997.

Mitchell, Barbara and Ormond. *Mitchell: The Life of W.O. Mitchell. The Years of Fame, 1948–1998*. Toronto: McClelland & Stewart, 2005.

Mitchell, Barbara and Ormond. *W.O.: The Life of W.O. Mitchell, Beginnings to* Who Has Seen the Wind *1914–1947*. Toronto: McClelland & Stewart, 1999.

Mitchell, W.O. *The Black Bonspiel of Willie MacCrimmon*. Illustrated by Wesley W. Bates. Toronto: McClelland & Stewart, 1993.

Mitchell, W.O. "Dear Mr. Manning ..." *An Evening with W.O. Mitchell*. Edited by Barbara and Ormond Mitchell. Toronto: McClelland & Stewart, 1997.

Mitchell, W.O. *Dramatic W.O. Mitchell*. Toronto: Macmillan of Canada, 1982.

Mitchell, W.O. "The People Who Don't Want Equality." *Maclean's*, July 3, 1965: 9.

ACKNOWLEDGEMENTS

We would like to thank the following for their help in our archival searches, in tracking down details for the productions of the two plays, and in arranging for permissions for the use of archival material, production photos and sketches: Brenda Carroll (CBC Image Research Library); Michael Moosberger and Kelly Casey (Dalhousie University Archives and Special Collections); Susan Kooyman and Lynette Walton (Glenbow Archives); Sharon Foley and M. Christopher Kotecki (Archives of Manitoba); Jonathan Davidson and Laurette Miller (Provincial Archives of Alberta); Appollonia Steele and Marlys Chevrefils (Special Collections, Information Resources, University of Calgary); Amy Gillingham (Archival and Special Collections, University of Guelph Library); Bob White, Amy Lynn Strilchuk, Meaghan Whitney, and Dianne Goodman (Alberta Theatre Projects); Joshua Semchuk (Citadel Theatre); Karen Jurzyniec (Globe Theatre); Deborah Harvey (Grand Theatre); Simon Day (Huron County Playhouse); Yvan LeBel (La Troupe du Jour); Tania Sigurdson, Laurie Lam and Zaz Bajon (Manitoba Theatre Centre); Doreen Malone and Mina Crandall (Neptune Theatre); Thomas Usher (Prime Stock Theatre Company); Natasha Nadir (Richmond Gateway Theatre); Judi Straughan (Sudbury Theatre Centre); Phyllis Bendig (Theatre Aquarius); Gillian Swan and Dennis Garnhum (Theatre Calgary); Greg Wanless and Kathryn MacKay (Thousand Islands Playhouse); Glynis Leyshon and Meredith Elliot (Vancouver Playhouse); Kevin McKendrick (Western Canada Theatre Company); Miriam Newhouse (Canadian Actors' Equity Association); Rick Chafe; Nancy Drake; Patricia Flood; Richard Gishler; Maxine Graham; Ann Harris; Violette Hiebert-Kelly; Ken Perchuk; Kathleen Ramsay; Douglas Riske; Tom Sheridan; Guy Sprung. We would also like to thank Jennie Rubio, our editor, and Katie Scott, our copy editor.

Every effort has been made to obtain permissions for use of the photographs from theatres, archives, artists, the Canadian Actors' Equity Association, and photographers.